SPIKE

MILLIGAN

A CELEBRATION

SPIKE MILLIGAN

A CELEBRATION

This edition first published in Great Britain in 2007 by
Virgin Books Ltd
Thames Wharf Studios
Rainville Road
London
W6 9HA

First published in Great Britain in 1995 by
Virgin Publishing Ltd

A catalogue record for this book is available from
the British Library.

ISBN 978 0 7535 1212 8

The paper used in this book is a natural, recyclable product
made from wood grown in sustainable forests. The
manufacturing process conforms to the regulations of the
country of origin.

Typeset by TW Typesetting, Plymouth, Devon
Printed and bound in Great Britain by
Mackays of Chatham Ltd, Kent

CONTENTS

INTRODUCTION

It was August 1966. I was working at ITV and I saw an advert in the paper for a personal assistant. I wanted to work somewhere near home and this was just around the corner from me, so I thought I'd give it a try for three months.

I told Spike I did not believe in contracts and anyway, I didn't want to sign anything I'd have to get out of when I wanted to go. We just shook hands on it and that was it.

Within that three months I'd become his manager. He had a manager at the time, but they had a row and Spike asked me to take on the job. It was really hectic with Spike and Eric Sykes and Frankie Howerd here – it was like working in a looney bin.

Once you got to know Spike, he was really quite easy to work with. It was a question of getting to know what he liked and what he disliked. That was the difficult bit.

There were good times and bad times. It was very upsetting when he was depressed and ill. He couldn't work then, but the people who knew him were very good – the people who didn't understand, I simply never worked with again. On the good side, he was a very stimulating man to work with . . . but he has been terribly underused.

People were apprehensive of him. He always said what he thought and some people didn't like that . . . but it is a simple fact that he paved the way for a new form of comedy . . . first with the 'Goon Shows' on radio and then with the 'Q' series on television. The 'Monty Python' people have always given him credit. They said that, without the 'Q' series and Spike, there never would have been a 'Monty Python'.

When he was given the Lifetime Achievement Award at the Comedy Awards, everyone stood up for him. They didn't do that for anyone else. I think in the business, people recognise what he has done. Personally, I think his writing is his dominant talent. Puckoon is the most extraordinarily funny book and I love his serious poetry.

He was an extraordinary man . . . he wrote, he painted, he composed songs. It really can make you feel a bit inadequate, but if you asked Spike how he would like to be remembered, he'd always say 'as a clown'.

Norma Farnes,
Spike Milligan's agent for over thirty years

THE SINGING FOOT
(A tale of a singing foot)

WOY WOY, AUSTRALIA. SEPTEMBER 1967

I have an uncle. His name is Herbert Jam. He was 52.
He worked in a laundry. One Christmas Eve he was
homeward bound on a crowded bus when he heard
what he thought was the sound of music coming from
inside his boot; indeed, what was to make him famous
had happened, his right foot had commenced to sing.
Poor Mr Jam tried to control the volume of sound by
tightening his boot lace; it only succeeded in making
the voice go from a deep baritone to a strangled tenor.
At the next stop Mr Jam had to get off. He walked
home to the sound of his right foot singing 'God rest
you merry Gentlemen', fortunately, Mr Jam knew the
words and mimed them whenever people passed by. It
was all very, very embarrassing. For three days he

stayed off work. His favourite TV programmes were ruined by unexpected bursts of song from the foot, he did manage to deaden it by watching with his foot in a bucket of sand, but, alas, from this practice he contracted a rare foot rot normally only caught by Arabs and camels. Worse was to come. The foot started singing at night. At three in the morning he was awakened with selections from 'The Gondoliers', 'Drake Is Going West' and 'A Whiter Shade of Pale'. He tried Mrs Helen Furg, a lady who was know to have exorcised Poltergeists and Evil Spirits, she tried a sprig of witchhazel round his ankle, intoned druidic prayers and burnt all his socks in the bath, but it wasn't long before the strains of 'The Desert Song' came lilting up his trouser leg again. On the recommendation of his doctor he visited the great Harley Street right-foot specialist, Sir Ralph Fees.

'Come in, sit down,' said the great man, 'Now what appears to be our trouble?'

'It's my right foot.'

'Of course it is,' said cheery Sir Ralph, 'and,' he went on, 'what appears to be the trouble with our right foot?'

'It sings.'

Sir Ralph paused (but still went on charging)

'You say your foot sings?'

'Yes it's a light baritone,' said wretched Jam. Sir Ralph started to write. 'I want you to go and see this Psychiatrist,' he said – at which very moment Uncle Herbert's foot burst into song! 'Just a minute,' said Sir Ralph, 'I'll get my hat and come with you.' The medical world and Harley Street were baffled. For the time being he had to make do with a surgical sound-proof boot and a pair of wax ear-plugs. Occasionally, he would take off his boot to give the lads at the Pub a song, but, Mr Jam was far from happy. Then came the beginning of the end, E.M.I. gave him a £500,000,000 contract for his foot to make records. A special group was formed, called 'The Grave', the billing was 'Mr Jam with One Foot in the Grave'. He was the news sensation of the year! But, it became clear that it was the right foot that got the fame, not Mr Jam. E.M.I. opened a bank account for the right foot. While his poor left foot wore an old boot his right foot wore expensive purple alligator shoes from Carnaby Street which cost £50 a toe. At parties he was ceaselessly taking off his shoe to sign autographs! Mr Jam was just an embarrassment to his right foot! One night in a fit of jealousy Mr Jam shot his foot through the instep. It never sang again! Mr Jam returned to the obscurity of his job in the laundry. He was 52, happy, only now he walked with a slight limp.

(From the book *The Bedside Milligan*, 1969)

OVERTURE

HQ Afrika Korps – Tunis January 1943. Smell of German ersatz eggs, sausages and Marlene Dietrich. A phone rings. General Stupenagel salutes it, and picks it up.

STUPENAGEL   Spielen!

GOERING   Do you know vere Von Rommel is? This is urgent.

STUPENAGEL   This is Von Urgent?

GOERING   Don't make wiz zer fuck-about! – vere is Rommel?

STUPENAGEL   He is in zer shit-house

GOERING   What is he doing in zere at zis time of zer morning?

STUPENAGEL   He is doing zer schitz, he was bombed all night.

GOERING   Donner Blitzen!

STUPENAGEL   He's in zer shit-house, too.

GOERING   Listen! Ve have had Bad News!

STUPENAGEL   Dat sounds like bad news!

GOERING   Our spy, Mrs Ethel Noss, in zer Algiers NAAFI, says dat zer Pritishers have brung zer heavy artillery into Africa.

STUPENAGEL   Gott no!

GOERING   Gott yes! Zey are going to make shoot bang-fire mit 200 pound shells.

STUPENAGEL   Oh, Ger-fuck!

GOERING   Tell Rommel, zer Fuhrer wants him to get mit zer Panzer and make vid zer Afrika Korps, Schnell!

Scene changes to a German latrine in a Wadi near Shatter-el-Arab. Stupenagel enters.

STUPENAGEL   Rommel, vich one are you in?

ROMMEL   Number Zeben.

STUPENAGEL   You must go to Tunis at once.

ROMMEL	Let me finish going here first.
STUPENAGEL	Zere is a crisis out zere.
ROMMEL	Zere is a crisis in in here; no paper (screams, sound of scratching)
STUPENAGEL	Vat is ger-wrong?
GOERING	Itchy Powder on zer seat!
STUPENAGEL	Ach zer Pritish Commandos have struck again.

(From the book *Rommel? Gunner Who?*, 1974)

POETRY

TERNS

Said the mother Tern
to her baby Tern
Would you like a brother?
Said baby Tern
to mother Tern
Yes
One good Tern
  deserves another.

THE FLEA

How teeny weeny wee
Is the teeny little flea.
But last night in my hotel
He made me scratch like merry hell!

(From the book *The Bedside Milligan*, 1969)

THE ABC

T'was midnight in the schoolroom
And every desk was shut
When suddenly from the alphabet
Was heard a loud 'Tut-tut!'

Said A to B, 'I don't like C;
His manners are a lack.
For all I ever see of C
Is a semi-circular back!'

'I disagree,' said D to B,
'I've never found C so.
From where *I* stand, he seems to be
An uncompleted O.'

C was vexed, 'I'm very much perplexed,
You criticise my shape.
I'm made like that, to help spell Cat
And Cow and Cool and Cape.'

'He's right,' said E; said F, 'Whoopee!'
Said G ' 'Ip, 'ip, 'ooray!'
'You're dropping me,' roared H to G.
'Don't do it please I pray!'

'Out of my way,' LL said to K.
'I'll Make poor I look ILL.'
To stop this stunt, J stood in front,
And presto! ILL was JILL.

'U know,' said V, 'that W
Is twice the age of me,
For as a Roman V is five
I'm half a young as he.'

X and Y yawned sleepily,
'Look at the time!' they said.
'Let's all get off to beddy byes.'
They did, then, 'Z-z-z.'

or
alternative last verse

X and Y yawned sleepily,
'Look at the time!' they said.
They all jumped into beddy byes
And the last one in was Z!

(From the book *The Little Pot Boiler*, 1963)

SIR HARRY SECOMBE CBE

As Eccles and Ned Seagoon – among many other characters – Spike and Sir Harry changed the face of British Comedy with the anarchic Goon Shows. The revolution had its beginnings in Naples in 1945, when a bunch of soldiers found they hadn't much to do at the end of World War Two.

The war was over and there were a lot of undemobbed troops. The Army was putting together shows to keep them entertained. We did auditions and joined a central pool of artists. I was in the barrack room and I heard Spike . . . and realised immediately that he was a fellow idiot!

Bill Hall was with me – he was a fiddler – and he started playing a bit. Spike joined in on guitar and Johnny Mulgrew was playing the bass. That was how the Bill Hall Trio was formed. I was the comic in the show they put together and there was an Italian starlet who provided the glamour. We toured around the country, playing shows.

Then I was demobbed, but Spike stayed on with the Bill Hall Trio until they were transported back to Britain.

I auditioned for the Windmill and Michael Bentine was there. I took him down to a pub called Graftons, in Westminster. Spike used to come down and he was eventually put up in an attic – we called him the Prisoner of Zenda.

We used to muck about with tape recorders and Peter Sellers joined at that time. Pat Dixon, a producer at the BBC, was always looking out for new twists of comedy ... he loved anarchic comedy.

We got a Goon Show script together. He gave us a pilot show and had us accepted. In those days, everyone chipped in with ideas, but eventually it was just Spike, trying to keep up this tremendous standard – it was what broke up his marriage and his health but he even carried on writing scripts from a mental home.

It was very exciting ... we used to really look forward to the Goons on a Sunday. It was like being let out of school. Peter would be in a film, I would be at the Palladium and it would be hysteria when we got together.

We would read through the script, do a run through with sound effects. Spike would watch us like a hawk to see our reactions to the script, then we'd just do it in the evening. We used to all get around one microphone until we got a bit larger and we had three microphones in the end! We were on the thermal currents of Spike's imagination – I felt privileged to be with him.

Spike is a very compassionate man and he has always espoused lost causes and is at the forefront of preserving them. He would always find something funny to say, but if something upset him, he would get up and walk out.

He hates noise. There are signs all over his house saying things like 'shut the door quietly'.

He came to stay with us in Cheam once and there was a large aquarium under his bedroom. The noise affected him so much that we found him the next day sleeping in the bath with a blanket over him!

Spike has definitely been underused – his unpredictability has frightened people off – but his anarchic style is needed. Cleese and Palin acknowledge they were influenced by us, because what we did was so different from anything that had gone before.

But Spike did suffer and his genius was overlooked. There was a senior producer at the BBC who once referred to the Goon Show, saying 'What exactly is this Go On Show?'

Spike is much misunderstood and undervalued. We ought to slap a preservation order on him. I'm very fond of the old bugger – we need him.

THE CALL OF THE WEST

It is 1867 and two dangerous criminals are on the run in the wild west of America. Grytpype-Thynne and Moriarty are wanted men, hunted by the US cavalry for selling saxophones to the Indians. With Moriarty disguised as a woman, they enter a saloon...

GRYTPYPE-THYNNE	I say, barman, drinks for my lady.
MORIARTY	I'll have a glass of Fish and Chips.
GRYTPYPE-THYNNE	And see you put a good head on it.
RAY	Man, we don't keep any drink called fish and chips
GRYTPYPE-THYNNE	Come, Moriarty, we'll take our trade and malnutrition elsewhere.

LT. HERN-HERN   Hold everything! I'm Lootenant Hern-Hern of the United States Cavalry, reasonable charges to regular customers ... Now we're looking for two men who've been selling contraband saxophones to the Red Injuns ... thereby causing unemployment among white musicians.

MORIARTY   Ohahahahoooooooo.

LT. HERN-HERN   (*suspicious*) Pardon me Ma'am, your ... a ... wig's fallen off.

GRYTPYPE-THYNNE   Wig? How dare you ... the unfortunate woman just happens to have gone bald suddenly ... it's obviously a case of the new lightning French alapecha ... from the song of the same name.

MORIARTY   That's right (*sings to tune of Aloetta*) 'Alapecha, lightning alapecha ... alapecha ... happens everyday.'

GRYTPYPE-THYNNE   (*sings*) 'First you get it on your nut' ...

MORIARTY   (*sings*) 'First you get it on your nut' ...

F.X. thwack

MORIARTY (*sings*) Ohh my nut . . .

GRYTPYPE-THYNNE (*sings*) Oh his nut . . .

MORIARTY (*sings*) Oh my nut.

**Orchestra Ooooooooooh . . .
Alapecha lightning alapecha . . .**

LT. HERN-HERN Woww . . . stop that alapecha . . . One moment you two . . . I seem to recognise your face Sir, take off that false nose . . . Ahha . . . now them false ears . . . now that false suit . . . now that false chest . . . just as I thought . . . I don't know who you are . . . Who are you?

GRYTPYPE-THYNNE Lord Nelson.

LT. HERN-HERN He had one arm missin'.

GRYTPYPE-THYNNE I have, I used to have three.

ECCLES Hello, Captain, care to join us for a hand of cards?

LT. HERN-HERN Poker, pontoon or rummy?

ECCLES Yer, yer . . . and cards.

CAPTAIN SLOKUM Alright fellas . . . I pass.

LT. HERN-HERN I pass.

ECCLES Mmmmmm . . . it's up to me now . . . I'm callin' you fellas.

BLUEBOTTLE Ooooh . . . he's calling us *all* fellas. It's the call of the West, partner . . . chews plug of Hopalong Cassidy cardboard string tobacco . . . spit spit spitee . . . ohh . . . it's gone right down the front of my shirt.

LT. HERN-HERN Who are you stranger? . . . Speak up!

BLUEBOTTLE I am . . . Marshall Matt Dillon . . . of 23 Flubb Ave . . . East Finchley North 12.

LT. HERN-HERN I ain't never seen you in Dodge city before . . . how did you get here?

BLUEBOTTLE I came on the 49 bus from the High Street.

LT. HERN-HERN There ain't no buses run out here.

BLUEBOTTLE No it only took me as far as the Odeon then I had to walk the rest of the way myself.

ECCLES What about the game?

LT. HERN-HERN OK, then you're calling Mad Dan. What kind of hand you got?

ECCLES   Four fingers and a thumb.

BLUEBOTTLE   I beat you Mad Dan . . . I got four fingers, two thumbs and a toe.

ECCLES   A toe? There ain't such a hand.

BLUEBOTTLE   Do you think I'm a cheat?

ECCLES   No, I think you're deformed.

BLUEBOTTLE   No man can call Bluebottle deformed unless he is a specialist . . . Eccles I'm running you in.

ECCLES   I've been run in. I've done ten thousand miles.

LT. HERN-HERN   Come on, Mad Dan . . . are you going quietly . . . or do we have to use ear plugs?

BLUEBOTTLE   Go for your guns, Mad Dan . . . I'm warning you – see the panther-like movement of my mittened hands as they curl towards the cardboard and string triggers of my cut-out pistol . . .

F.X. door opens

BLUEBOTTLE'S MUM   There you are, you dirty little tramp . . .

BLUEBOTTLE	Oooh, Mum . . .
BLUEBOTTLE'S MUM	I'll give you 'oh, Mum'. . . your father's been looking everywhere for his trilby hat . . . Where's all the shopping I sent you for?

F.X. Slapsticks

BLUEBOTTLE	(*Over above*) Oh, mum, you've spoilt my game . . . ooh . . . bye bye Eccles.

(From Goon Show 254 first broadcast on 20 January 1959)

PUCKOON

Gulio Caesar presents The World's Finest Animal Circus. The words were painted six foot high in modest black and white. Circus master Gulio Caesar, 'King of the ring', was a worried man. Constantly at war with fleas that continually transferred their allegiance from the monkeys to him, he slept with a tin of Keatings by his bed. At midnight he awoke scratching and cussing, when through his caravan window he made the awful discovery. The cage was open and the beast had gone. Scratching with one hand and dialling with the other, he phoned the RSPCA.

Awakening from his veterinary slumbers, Inspector Felix Wretch groped in the dark for the jangling instrument.

'Hello?'

This is a – Gulio Caesar, could I please spik wid your husband?'

'Me husband speaking,' said Mr Wretch.

'Gooda, one of my black-a panthers has escape.'

Mr Wretch gulped himself into consciousness, 'I'll meet you outside the police station right away in ten minutes.'

'Right,' the line clicked to immutability.

Hurriedly Mr Wretch pocketed a humane killer, a phial of liquid and a hypodermic, then stepped into his trousers and into the night.

Into the wood along the river bank stumbled five happy drunks. Suddenly Rafferty stopped.

'Shhh, there's something in me trap,' he said excitedly.

The information silenced the singing. Cautiously they approached towards a black sheep crouching on the ground.

'It's a – ' commenced Rafferty, but was cut short by a scarlet mouth emitting an unusually loud growl. 'No, it isn't,' he concluded

'It isn't what?' queried O'Brien.

'It isn't what I thought it was at first.'

'Oh?'

'It should,' went on Rafferty, peering at the creature, 'it should be a fox.' The creature repeated a loud growl enough to stop the five in their tracks. What it was they knew not, that it was very big they knew, but what type of big they also knew not.

'I don't tink it's a goat,' Milligan said.

'You're right,' agreed Dr Goldstein. 'It's the wrong noise for a goat, if it was a goat it would go –' (he draw a big breath) 'BAAAAAAAAAAA, BAAAAAAAAAA.'

'For God's sake keep quiet, Doctor,' said Rafferty, who for the first time in his poaching life was puzzled.

'BBBBBBBBBBBAAAAAAAA!' continued Goldstein. Kneeling on all fours he charged O'Brien's unsuspecting seat.

'What in h –' O'Brien started to say as he fell forward. There was an inky black pause and a great splash. 'You bloody Jewish idiot!' said O'Brien, wallowing-groping-stumbling-falling in the shallow river waters. 'Gis yer hand,' said O'Mara pulling the soggy O'Brien to the bank.

'Feel if dere's any fish in his pockets,' said the Milligan holding his stomach with laughter.

'Shhhhhhhhh!' said Rafferty.

'I'll get you for dis, Goldstein,' said O'Brien. They were all silenced by a low, almost evil, snarl from the beast. Rafferty took a coil of rope from his sack. 'Here, little animal,' he said advancing cautiously. The reply was a stomach-loosening roar. Rafferty stooped uneasily and walked back to the arguing, singing group. 'A thought just struck me,' said Rafferty. 'Is dere any wild wolves left in Ireland?'

'Now I think I can answer that,' said Goldstein, 'Will someone strike a light?'

Milligan struck a match as the doctor read from a small pocket encyclopaedia, unsteadily flicking the pages.

'Ahhhh!', he said. 'Listen, dere are no wild wolves left in Ireland. The last one was killed in 1785 in MacGillikudie's Reeks by German naturalist called Herman Von Loon. Oh,' he read on, 'here's another bit of interesting data. In 1794 a black man called Talmadge Frock crossed Ireland on a wooden roller skate and died of leg cramps. He ...' Darkness followed a yell as the match burnt Milligan's finger.

'What about gettin' this animal, I'm gettin' cold,' O'Brien said.

Rafferty beckoned them all towards the beast. 'I'll get this noose over his neck, den everyone take one leg each.'

They advanced unsteadily. 'Puss, puss, puss,' said the Milligan, holding out his hand.

'You're right, Milligan, it's a cat, a black cat. Gad, he's had a good feed, look at the size of him.'

The animal sprang, uprooting the trap, hitting O'Mara in the chest. O'Mara the giant got to his feet.

'No bloody pussy-cat's going to do that to me.' He lashed out, struck the animal a pole-axe blow, and the panther sank into unconsciousness.

The five split up. O'Mara paused only once on the way, to throw a struggling panther into the charge room in the police station. There followed a series of ripping, growls and screams, then came a shattering of glass as the night constable dived through the window and ran up the road.

Two little men with the arse out of their trousers were holding a mass meeting. They had both known better days but not partaken in them. They were forced to admit that the glorious days of the IRA were in decline.

'Comrades,' said Shamus Ford, addressing his partner from a chair, 'I have good tidings. This new Customs Post at Puckoon is a boon and a blessing to men. I have a plan, such a plan as Brian Boru would be glad to be associated in.'

Looking at him, adoringly, was the sad, middle-aged, unshaven little face of the faithful follower,

Lenny Braddock. He scratched himself furiously, at the same time giving off a few supporting 'Hear hears'. Shamus banged his mittened hands across his body. The deserted barn was draughty, dirty, and dungy, but rent free. Shamus went on with great fire:

'To bury the stiffs dese days, they'se got to takes 'em through dat new Customs Post, it's a gift from heaven, don't you see?'

'No, I don't see, Shamus.'

'Pay attention den, gi's a puff on yer fag ... ta ... Our contacts on the other side says they're short of explosives. Right?'

'If you say so ...'

'I do. Now normally, without the convenience of a coffin, you'd have yer luggage searched and yer pockets.'

That's true, that's true ... can I have me fag back?'

'Now. If we could get a coffin and rig up a phony burial, we could carry enough gelignite stuff in dat coffin to blow Ulster back into the Republic – you see?'

'Gor! By gor! Dat is a fine plan boyo! A fine plan! I fink this is a turning point in the history of Ireland. Can I have me fag back?'

Wot we need is a coffin – don't snatch like that.'

'Me fag –'

'A coffin! Now dere's a mortician in Delarose Street ... you got them counterfeit pound notes? Good.'

'Can I have me fag back?'

'Of course, we got to make the plan watertight.' Shamus reclined back on his straw throne.

'Tomorrow I'll make arrangements fer der coffin.'

Suddenly, it was tomorrow. 'God, doesn't time fly?' said Shamus.

A recently lacerated constable with a finely shredded seat to his trousers addressed Mr Gulio Caesar. 'Have you lost a black panther, sir?'

'Yes, I have – she's-a-gone. Disastro!'

'I think I have made contact with the animal.'

The constable described his flight from fur-covered death. 'The animal is lurking in the wood a mile south of the church of St Theresa.'

'Mama mia! My porra panther – me and Mr Wretch will get there at a-once.'

'At once,' repeated Mr Wretch, loading his hypodermic.

They set off with a horse-drawn cage and a plentiful supply of drugged meat. It was dangerous for a panther to wander alone in Ireland. Once in paleolithic ages great dinatrons roamed the Celtic swamps. They had become extinct not of evolutionary process; there were O'Maras alive in those times, too.

In six months from recruitment, Ah Pong had picked up an amount of the language and could write a report on simple Irish crimes – murder, rape etc. Kitted out in blue, he was given a warrant and entrained to Puckoon. Appearing at the door of Puckoon Police Station, he was arrested on sight.

'Constable Oaf, you've been drinking,' MacGillikudie had accused him.

'Me not Constable Oaf,' said the little Chinese.

'Then I arrest you for-for-you!' The accompanying letter was hard to believe. From the Commissioner of Police? He must be off his nut! A Chinese policeman in exchange for Oaf? 'I don't suppose it's a bad swop,' he reflected.

He found Ah Pong a very willing worker, and therefore gave him the lot. Clever people these Chinese. Sax Rohmer had said so, he should know, he was one of them. He kept Ah Pong on night duty. He explained his reasons. 'Got to break it to the people gentlemanlike,' that and the other reason, a hungry panther loose.

The world had so many Chinese they wouldn't miss this one.

Passing the station one day, Rafferty had dropped in to see if there were any warrants out for his arrest. He entered. Ah Pong had his back to the door.

'Good morning, Sarge,' said Rafferty cheerfully. Ah Pong turned. 'Please?' he said. The little Chinaman advanced towards Rafferty.

'Don't come near me, MacGillikudie, I don't want to catch it.'

'Please, what-is-trouble? said Ah Pong.

I was right, thought Rafferty, dat was a Chinese I saw the other night.

'Where's Sergeant MacGillikudie?' he asked.

'Sergeant asleep.'

'Does he know you're wearing his uniform?'

'Please understand, I real police, my name Ah Pong.'

He held out his hand and shook Rafferty's.

'You're a real polis?'

'Look.' Ah Pong put on his helmet, pointed one finger in the air, and blew his whistle. 'See?'

Rafferty paused, his lips pursed. His face took on a cunning look.

'Do you know the meaning of the word poacher?'

'Sorry, me no understand.'

Rafferty's face burst into a smile. 'Me and you is going to get on real fine.' He shook the smiling Chinaman's hand and departed. Ah Pong opened a Chinese-English dictionary and ran his finger down the Ps, p-o-a-c-h-e-r. Ahhhh!

He made a swift note in Pekinese. Soon Rafferty was to know the meaning of the word 'Inscrutable'.

(From the book *Puckoon*, 1963)

DENIS NORDEN

Denis Nordern and Spike met in the days when their new and innovative type of comedy was bursting onto the radio scene. Denis Nordern is a great admirer of Spike's not only as a comedian but as writer of comic verse and classic lines such as 'Anybody can be 52, but it takes a bus to be 52b'. He agrees with many others, when he says that being in the theatre with Spike could be an unpredictable experience ... even when you were just a member of the audience!

We were part of the group that was emerging at that time. It was completely non-competitive and there had been no radio comedy of the kind we were envisaging. There were loads of people bursting to do things with it. The more any one of us succeeded, the better it was for all of us. It could be a great strain, writing 26 shows in a season and there was a lot of swapping of ideas and appeals for help.

Spike is an authentic comedy genius, along with Eric Sykes and Sid Field, but he has not received the official recognition that he deserves. There are a lot of raincoat manufacturers out there, walking around with titles . . . but Spike isn't. Within the trade, he's very well known – and all the American comedians know him. The people up above should acknowledge him.

He has the gift of doing very complex ideas in a very lucid and economical way – people who do comedy for a living are constantly amazed at that. The Python boys, Ben Elton and people like that . . . they all bow to him.

He's also one of the best writers of comic verse we've ever had, but he isn't recognised for that. I am a great fan of his poems, particularly 'Silly Verse For Kids'. My children would just absorb them . . . and now they are reading them to their children.

Spike got through to children in a way no-one else could. He presented 'Children's Choice' – playing records and talking to the kids. All my children and their schoolmates would listen to it.

'I remember he was in a play in the West End called 'Oblomov'. It was an excuse for ad-libbing and he changed the lines every night. The rest of the cast had the obligation of sticking to their lines, but Spike just stalked through the play doing what he wanted.

I went to see the play one night and – unfortunately – Spike spotted me in the audience. He just stopped and said to me 'Come on, Denis, you're a comedy writer – what should I say next'?

'This went on throughout the play. I would come up with an idea – he would pour scorn on it and he even got me to sing!

POETRY

RAIN

There are holes in the sky
Where the rain gets in,
But they're ever so small
That's why the rain is thin.

(From the book *Silly Verse For Kids*, 1959)

THE Q SERIES

NEWSDESK

SPIKE   Good evening. Welcome to Q6, the show that keeps the rain off.

Adjacent to Spike is a Newsdesk. On it is a parcel. He walks to the desk, shows he is wearing no trousers.

SPIKE   It's from Princess Anne. (*Opens box and reads card*) 'Spike Darling, I always send you one of these when you do a TV series, wear it for me.'

He takes awful false nose from box. Puts it on.

SPIKE   Isn't Royalty wonderful? Thanks Anne. And Mark, don't take it too bad, you've always got the horses.

A front door. Next to it a man is strangling a man while a second man hits him on the head. Man being strangled wears a Princess Anne gift nose.

POLICEMAN   Mrs Terrible?

WOMAN   Yes.

POLICEMAN   Wife of Ivan Terrible, the one who works on the oil rigs in dangerous shark infested waters during raging force 9 gales?

WOMAN   Yes . . . is it bad news?

POLICEMAN   Yes, very bad . . . my wife's run off with a burgler (*Cries*).

WOMAN   There, there, I'll give you some good news . . . Princess Anne will be 25 on the 15th August.

POLICEMAN   I do believe I feel better already. (*Looks at men strangling each other*). I wonder if these men know Princess Anne will be 25 on the 15th August. Do you know these people?

WOMAN   The one that's being strangled is my lodger. I don't know the other two.

Policeman blows whistle. The two assailants immediately shout.

ASSAILANT   Look out . . . he's got a whistle.

They run to corner and take out their own whistles. There follows a whistle battle, peeping round corner and blowing. Cut back to policeman hiding in doorway blowing his whistle back. Several more police whistles are heard approaching. They all take up whistle blowing positions.

ASSAILANT   Don't blow any more copper, we give up.

POLICEMAN   Throw out your whistles and come out with yer hands over your ears.

The assailants throw their whistles in, and come out with hands over ears.

POLICEMAN   (*to camera*) But I had made a grave mistake. These two men were in fact plainclothes policemen, and they were apprehending a plainclothes criminal.

Original man who is being strangled speaks.

MAN   (*to camera*) Yes, you see, I am six feet tall but I was in a five feet nine zone.

POLICEMAN   Therefore, I cautioned him so (*turns to man*): Sir you are exceeding the legal height by inches three.

MAN   I want to see a lawyer.

Policeman hands him a telescope that he immediately clasps to his eye.

POLICEMAN   There's one in that window up there.

Cut to a courtroom. The whole court is built crushed together. The Judge's box is almost on top of the witness box in which is the accused, suspended by a kirby wire that can pull him up, in the upright position. He wears a long raincoat that will be about twenty feet long. The desired effect is that when he is hoisted twenty feet, the coat will unfold, the bottom half still on the floor of the witness box. The accused wears a Princess Anne gift nose. The defending counsel wears a Princess Anne gift nose.

DEFENCE   M'lud my client admits being six foot in a five foot nine area.

All the cast go into overacted mumbles of surprise.

JUDGE   (*bangs desk with mallet that breaks in two*) Silence, I will not have overacting in my court. (*Looks at camera and smiles.*)

DEFENCE   I appeal to camera three, my client claims mitigating circumstances. He was drunk and lost control of his height.

JUDGE	Did you get a doctor's report?
DEFENCE	No, we got a builder's estimate.
JUDGE	Why?
DEFENCE	It was cheaper, and can a lady with a wooden leg change a pound note?
JUDGE	Yes.
DEFENCE	No.
JUDGE	Why not?
DEFENCE	She's only got half a nicker.

Colossal burst of canned laughter.

JUDGE	Silence, I will not have canned laughter in my court. (*Returns to Judge character.*) Now, will you explain why your client is wearing that ridiculous nose?
DEFENCE	He's in love with Princess Anne, your Hon.
JUDGE	Is that why you're wearing one?
DEFENCE	Yes M'Lud.
JUDGE	Why's yours bigger?
DEFENCE	I've known her longer.
JUDGE	Ronald Biggs, of no fixed trousers, you are accused of being illegally tall in Lewisham. How do you plead?

ACCUSED   I plead like this

**Immediately snow starts to fall next to him in the box a poverty stricken woman with black headshawl holding a bundle stands up and cries.
Music: Theme from Tchaikovsky's 'Romeo and Juliet' ...**

ACCUSED   (*goes into terrible overacting sadness*) I've got a wife and ten kids and she's in the club again. I was at Dunkirk, I had it shot off ...

JUDGE   I'm sorry, your plea has failed to get the maximum number of points. Ronald Biggs, inside leg 32, I sentence you to be hung by the neck until you are inside leg 37.

Here he is hauled up twenty feet shouting.

ACCUSED   I am innocent, innocent!

DEFENCE   My client has gone to a higher court.

(From the book *Q Annual*, 1969)

JIM DALE

The actor, Jim Dale, has some vivid memories of Spike Milligan – including fields full of cows and The Unsinkable Duck. They shared a manager at one time and worked together on a film, 'Digby – the Biggest Dog in the World.' But Jim Dale can also claim that he *was* Spike, playing him in the film version of 'Adolf Hitler – My Part In His Downfall.'

The first time I ever went into Spike's office, I remember immediately noticing a picture of a duck on the picture rail on the wall. The wall below it was painted blue with fish and other underwater scenes – the picture rail was supposed to be the surface of the water.

The duck had one little foot paddling just below the surface of the water – the picture rail – but the other foot was eight feet long and stretched right down to the floor. Spike had called it The Unsinkable Duck!

Being offered the role of Spike Milligan made me feel a bit apprehensive – I was worried how the critics, the public and Spike himself would think of the the portrayal.

I had to set out to do a copy of what Spike was like at the time described in the book – not what everyone thought he was like when we made the film. I had to get over the stupidity of the Army and Spike having to play a part in something totally against his nature – war.

We had to show the silly things that Spike was doing at the time. We went through the book very carefully to try to recreate the drawings that Spike had done – especially of him in his uniform. In the American Army, they shaved your head to make you inferior – in England they just gave you an outrageously large uniform that didn't fit . . . even the ties didn't fit!

The ability to lie in a field surrounded by cows is something Spike taught me . . . and I'm eternally grateful to him for it. He told me that if you crawl into the field on all fours and quietly lie down, the cows will come over and touch you. They're not frightened because they've never seen a man on all fours before. I tried it in Scotland. I crawled into the field and lay down and the cows all came and stood around me. The cows nuzzle you, touching your face and they're so gentle. I thought 'thank you Spike – it's a lovely experience' – until I saw one of the 'cows' had two huge balls hanging underneath. I was out of the field over a gate in no time!

Spike has influenced the minds of people outside showbusiness as well as inside it. When people have needed a comic nudge in the ribs to get them thinking, Spike has had the comic ability to bring the matters to the fore. It's only when you've laughed at what he's said that you realise that what he was talking about was not funny in itself. He's got the ability to get through to people through comedy. I have great admiration for him.

BARRACK ROOM HUMOUR

What I am about to relate is bawdy and vulgar but as it's true it stands on its own merits.

It was after lights out that some of the most hysterical moments occurred. Those who had been drinking heavily soon made it known by great asphyxiating farts that rendered their owners unconscious and cleared the beds all around. There were even more gentlemen who performed feats with their unwanted nether winds that that not even the great Petomane could have eclipsed; simply, they set fire to them. The 'artiste' would bend down, his assistant stood by with a lighted match. When the 'artiste' let off he ignited it. Using this method I have seen sheets of blue flame up to a foot in length. Old timers, by conserving their fuel, could scorch a Tudor Rose on the wall. There was Signaller 'X' whose control of the anal sphincter allowed him to pass morse code messages. With my own ears I heard him send S.O.S. On these occasions I, like others, lay in bed crying with laughter. But the most unbelievable 'act' was Gunner 'Plunger' Bailey, who did an entire twenty minute act with his genitals.

It was done on a very professional basis. After lights out a gunner would use a torch as a spot light, which lit the 'artiste's' genitals: the third member of the act, Bill Hall, sang 'Bird Song at Eventide' as the star manipulated his genitals to look like 'Sausage On A Plate', 'The Last Turkey In The Shop', 'Sack Of Flour', 'The Roaring Of The Lions', and by using spectacles 'Groucho Marx'. Finally for the National Anthem he made the member stand. Each manipulation was received with a storm of clapping and cries of 'Encore'.

Snoring. Each one had his own unique sound. Gunner Forest's was like gargling with raw eggs through a gently revolving football rattle. For sheer noise, Gunner Notts. He vibrated knives, forks and spoons on the other side of the room. Before he went to sleep we secured all the loose objects with weights. Syd Price gave off snores so vibrant his bed travelled up to six inches a night. On bad nights we'd find it out in the passage. Next, the teeth grinders! Gunner Leech's was like a dry cork twisting in the neck of a bottle, followed by the word, 'Fissssssshhhhhhh!'

This next story was passed on from A Sub-section, stationed at Alfriston. The gun crew were billited in a beautiful old inn. The men were given the whole length of the attic. At one end was the Great Gun Bucket that gunners place in their midst for use in inclement weather. It was worth its weight in gold, but there were the 'Spoilers'. Those men, when the tub was full, would sneak up in the dark and silently 'relieve' themselves: this caused 'spillage', and gradually, without their knowledge, the floor and the ceiling underneath were starting to rot. Came the terrible night, when Lieutenant Sebag-Montefiore, sleeping soundly below, was awakened by the sound of the ceiling falling through on him, followed by some twenty gallons of well-matured urine.

There was a hell of a row, the landlord demanded compensation, etc, etc. The ceiling was made good, the Gunners reprimanded, and it all blew over, all except the smell. For months after – if you were down wind – you could always tell where Lieutenant Sebag-Montefiore was.

(From the book *Adolph Hitler: My Part In His Downfall*, 1971)

RONNIE SCOTT

As well as his genius for comedy, Spike had another great talent – music. With it went a deep-rooted love of jazz . . . which naturally led him to the most famous jazz club around – Ronnie Scott's in the West End. Spike and Ronnie Scott struck up a friendship based on their mutual interest in comedy and music, about which Spike had the odd unusual insight . . . particularly where Beethoven was concerned.

He first came into the club about 25 years ago. He's into jazz and plays all sorts of instruments himself. He knew I admired him, he's an easy person to talk to and it went from there.

He had his own special table at the club in the corner and used to come along quite a lot – depending on who was playing.

He's been a very good friend to me over the years, particularly some years ago, when I was not well. He used to send taxis to take me to his house and he helped me out financially as well.

I did something on one of his shows and took part in various shows about him, including 'This Is Your Life'.

Most musicians loved 'The Goon Show' and they love Spike – he has their type of humour. I've always found him a warm and generous man, as well as being funny. I think he's a genius and has had an enormous influence. All good comedians and shows have been influenced by him – and if they haven't; they should be. He's innovative, witty and very irreverent.

There's one story about him I'll always remember, which shows all that. It was when I wasn't well – he took me to the Albert Hall to see Beethoven's Heroica. It was in the third movement of the concert, which is a funeral march. It's very slow and solemn – a wonderful piece of music but it does go on a bit.

Spike was listening to it, but he eventually turned to me and said: 'This bloke must have lived a fucking long way from the cemetery.'

THE RASPBERRY SONG

In a little town where I belong,
There's a most accomplished fellow.
He's the leader of the village choir,
And his voice is warm and mellow.
He drives a fruit cart round the street
And everybody knows it:
He doesn't sing or rave about
His fruit, he simply blows it

XXX XXX XXX XXX XXX – 'raspberry'

He's doing it all day long

XXX XXX XXX XXX XXX

It's better than any song,
Though it isn't very pretty
You've got to admit it's cute
So, all together, let it go

XXX XXX XXX XXX XXX

It's certainly come to stay

XXX XXX XXX XXX XXX

It's a treat to hear him say, 'Hey
Fruit's in season, plenty there is:
Apples, plums and the old raspberries

XXX XXX XXX XXX XXX

Everything is fresh today.'

Every Friday night when work is done,
He never wastes a minute.
To the village hall he hurries round
Where he sings just like a linnet.

To hear him blow a melody
It's great you can't deny it;
And if you've got nothing else to do
I'd like you all to try it.

XXX XXX XXX XXX XXX

Get ready and do it now.

XXX XXX XXX XXX XXX

It's easy when you know how.
Though it isn't very pretty
You've got to admit it's cute
So, all together, let it go

XXX XXX XXX XXX XXX

Eat more fruit

XXX XXX XXX XXX XXX

It's certainly come to stay

XXX XXX XXX XXX XXX

It's a treat to hear him say, 'Hey
So Te La So Fa Me Re Doh

XXX XXX XXX XXX XXX

Everything is fresh today!'

It's certainly come to stay

XXX XXX XXX XXX XXX

It's a treat to hear him say
Fruit's in season, plenty there is:
Apples, plums and old raspberries

XXX XXX XXX XXX XXX

Everything is fresh today!

SUN HELMET

A pleasant three degrees below zero wind was blowing. The early morning Londoners shivered through the bitingly cold rush hour. Among them was a bowler-hatted Mr Oliver Thrigg. The first snow of summer was starting to fall as he joined his 'AA members only' bus cue. Glancing to a bus que opposite (it was a different que to his cue, as the spelling proves), and what he saw shook him to his foundation garment. There, in the que opposite, was a man wearing a sun helmet, eccentricity yes, but this fellow didn't have a stamp of a genuine eccentric, no, fellow looked far too normal! Curiosity got the upper hand, crossing the road he killed a cat. Once across he joined the que and left his on the other side. The sun-helmeted man caught a 31A bus, Mr Thrigg signalled a passing 49A. 'Follow that bus,' he told the driver.

'Anywhere but Cuba,' said the driver. At Victoria Station the sun-helmeted man booked to Southampton, as did Mr Thrigg, who kept him under surveyaliance until they reached Southampton, where by now the snow was 3 foot deep, which explained the absence of dwarfs in the street. The man continued to wear his sun helmet. 'Why, why, why,' said Thrigg whose curiosity had killed another nine cats, making a grand total of one. 'I must follow this man etc.' The man booked aboard the Onion Castle and was handed £10 and an oar (Assisted Passage they call it). The ship headed south, and, so did Mr Thrigg and his enigma, which he used for colonic irrigation. During the whole trip the man appeared at all times in a sun helmet. Several or eightal times he was almost tempted to ask the man his secret. But no, as Thrigg was travelling steerage and the man 1st class, plus the fact it was a special Non-fraternising Apartheid Cruise, no contact was possible. On the 12th of Iptomber the ship docked at Cape Town. Even though Thrigg got through Customs and Bribes at speed, he just missed the Sun Helmet as he drove in a taxi. Thrigg flagged down an old cripple Negro driver 'Follow that Sun Helmet' he said jumping on the nigger's back. (The change from Negro to Nigger denotes change from UK to SA soil.) Several times Thrigg let the nigger stand in his bucket of portable UK soil so he could be called Negro. To cut the story short, Mr Thrigg used scissors and cornered the man in the middle of the Sahara. The heat was intolerable as Thrigg walked up and said 'Why are you wearing that sun helmet?' 'Because,' said the man, pointing at a 113 thermometer in the shade, 'the sun man! This protects the head.' 'I see,' said Mr Thrigg. 'Well I better be off, I'm late for work.' As he departed for the caravan que, the man in the sun helmet spotted him. 'Good God, a man wearing a bowler hat! A bowler hat? Here, in the Sahara? I must find out why,' he thought as he joined the caravan cue behind Mr Thrigg.

(From the book *The Bedside Milligan*, 1969)

THE ARREST OF A WITCH

A police station with a few sparse
Christmas decorations. Sergeant
stands behind desk, next to an open
window. He is polishing his
truncheon and talking to himself.

SERGEANT   I would've got him for trespassing and
wilful damage . . .

Sounds of woman's screams and
struggle outside window. He shuts
window.

SERGEANT   We'll have to join the Noise
Abatement Society. Now then . . . no
one about . . . (*He takes plastic bust of
bearded male hippy from underneath
desk and places it on top*) . . . take
that . . . (*He hits bust with truncheon*)
you 'orrible 'airy 'ippy. (*He hits bust*

again) and that, you guitar playing layabout. (*Continues to hit bust while abusing it*) and take that, for getting more money than me with those silly pop songs and me with my lovely baritone (*Sings*). And that . . . and that . . . (*Now starts strangling bust, while growling and shouting*).

Sees another policeman come in. He quickly puts bust back under desk, and pretends to be working. A young policeman enters wearing a huge pink pig's nose and pair of ears.

SERGEANT   (*Looks puzzled*) Constable Shagnasty, you're drunk.

CONSTABLE   No, I'm not Sarge, I . . .

SERGEANT   Yes you are, take that silly pig's hooter off and them elephant lugs.

CONSTABLE   I can't, they're real.

SERGEANT   What are you talking about they're real?

CONSTABLE 1   I arrested a witch and she put a spell on me, Sarge.

Another constable enters leading a witch in a pointy hat, and carrying her broomstick.

CONSTABLE 2   It's true Sarge. (*Hands broom stick to Constable 1*)

SERGEANT   A witch! (*Standing up*) I never heard such rubbish in all my life.

CONSTABLE 1   Exhibit A (*Lifting broomstick to show Sergeant*) To whit.

SERGEANT   (*Indignant*) Who's a twit?

CONSTABLE 1   (*Pointing at broomstick*) This proves it.

SERGEANT   That proves he's a twit? Good. (*Writes this down*)

CONSTABLE 1   I stopped her as she was riding it down Oxford Street.

SERGEANT   Yes. (*examining broomstick*)

CONSTABLE 1   I discovered the broomstick was untaxed and unlicenced.

SERGEANT   Keep going.

CONSTABLE 1   She said she was in a hurry. I told her to take a taxi. She refused, smashed the taxi driver's window. Kapow, blatt, slam!!

SERGEANT   Oh, and does he wish to press charges?

CONSTABLE 1   Yeah, I'll get him. (*Leaves stage right*)

SERGEANT   Now listen, Madam, I must warn you that anything you say will be taken down and used in evidence. (*Jabs finger at witch who cackles. Constable 2 shys away.*)

WITCH   Eye of newt and leg of toad.

SERGEANT   Right . . . (*begins to write*) eye of newt and leg of . . . what was that last animal?

WITCH   Toad . . . (*graciously begins to spell this*) T . . . O . . .

SERGEANT   I know, I know, T . . . O . . . D . . . E, I'm no Z Car copper, you know.

Constable 1 re-enters holding hands with a chimpanzee, who is wearing trousers and an anorak.

SERGEANT   What's this then?

CONSTABLE 1   It's a cabbie.

SERGEANT   No, it's not it's a bleeding monkey.

CONSTABLE 1   Well she put a spell on him an' all, Sarge.

SERGEANT   What?! I've had enough of you, darling. (*Steps down from behind desk, taking bunch of keys off hook.*) I'm taking you and putting you in the cooler for the night.

He takes witch by hand and leads her off stage left. We hear the clanking of cell doors being locked. When the sergeant returns he has the head of a bull.

SERGEANT   That put an end to her little game.

The two constables and the chimpanzee are staring dumb-struck at the sergeant with his bull's head.

SERGEANT   What are you looking at? What's that matter with you?

(From the BBC TV Christmas Special 'Milligan In Winter', 1972)

SPIKE'S LETTERS

Spike has always been a prolific letter writer, whether keeping in touch with friends, speaking out on important issues or simply offering advice and sympathy . . .

1. Pauline Jones was sent to prison for abducting a baby out of love – not for money.

25th January 1972

Dear Pauline Jones,

I am just writing to tell you that I don't think that you should be put in any kind of prison, I think it very cruel that they should do this to you, and many thousands of people think the same. I admit you must have given great mental anguish to the parents but you were so desperate to love something that you did not think of that.

If there is anything I can get you while you are in prison like books or magazines, do let me know.

Love, light and Peace,

SPIKE MILLIGAN

2. He could not find out if she received his letters or not. He wrote to several people including Miss Morgan – the Governor of the prison.

22nd March 1972

Dear Miss Morgan,

Thank you for your letter of the 17th March.

I cannot help thinking this is ambiguous in that, and I quote, 'Pauline Jones received all the correspondence she was entitled to'. Therefore, was my correspondence among that which she was entitled to? If not, what happens to a letter written to a prisoner, to which she is not entitled – is the letter destroyed or is it returned to the sender?

All I am trying to do is to make contact with this girl to try and help her, and I am sure you will agree that this is a good thing. So in trying to help her I am seeking your help to inform me as to whether she received my letter, and has she read it.

You do appreciate my approach is a humanitarian one and your reply did not answer my question in my first letter. So I wonder if you could be more specific. It is very simple to say yes or no, because if she has not received my letter quite obviously I must write to her again.

Once again, this can only be done when I have received sufficient information from you.
Sincerely,

SPIKE MILLIGAN

3. He persisted.

23rd March 1972

Dear Pauline,

I have already written one letter to you but you may not have got it because, as you mentioned in the press, you were not getting all the mail you should.

I wrote to the Governor of Askham Grange who answered me in ambiguous terms saying you had got all the mail you were entitled to. So I am writing again in the hope that you get this letter.

I wrote saying that I disagreed entirely with having you put away in any kind of Institution, and I believe you should have a home atmosphere with lots of love and

understanding and tolerance. I still
believe this is the case and I said so
specifically on 'Speak Easy' last Sunday
and everybody in the audience agreed with
me. If you do get this letter I beg of you to
answer it just so I know that you have got
it. I will keep writing to you until I get an
answer.

If you cannot write to me, can you ask one
of your prison visitors to telephone me at
London and tell me whether you are getting
any mail from me?

If there is anything I can do to help you
in any way please let me know and I will do
my best.

Love, Light, and Peace,

SPIKE MILLIGAN

To: The Governor
H. M. Prison
Styal
29th September 1972

Dear Sir,

Here is a book of poems that I would like to
give to Pauline Jones. However, I believe
there are prison rules which sometimes
restrict the handing on of books or
presents to persons. If this should be the
case, I should like the book to be returned
to me in the attached envelope. Though for

the love of me I cannot imagine what possible harm the book can do to the prison system, other than make it more human.

Respectfully

SPIKE MILLIGAN

Finally he managed to make contact with her, and received several letters from her. Here are two of the letters he wrote to her.

5th July 1972

My dear Pauline,

Owing to pressure of work I am dictating this letter to you, whereas I would prefer to write it by hand. We are living in a mad world.

I was delighted to see that, rather than sitting around feeling sorry for yourself, you have got stuck into something called by that good old name 'work'. Believe me, Pauline, people are not very fond of working these days, but usually those people are miserable and dissatisfied because of that very reason.

My mother is 78 now, she gets up at 6.30 in the morning and three days a week she goes to Mass, she cleans the house herself, washes all the sheets by hand, looks after the garden and makes jam preserves, and I really don't know of a happier woman.

I myself when I am very depressed work as hard as I can and as well as I can, and but for that I think I would go mad. So remember this as a fellow neurotic work is almost Godlike.

The fact that you have learned to crochet and upholster means that if you cared to you could set yourself up in one room and sell it to the numerous boutiques that are springing up in London that are looking for quality work and unusual items.

Five months and nine days, of course, seems a long time to somebody in prison, and to somebody outside not long at all, this quite obviously is a frame of mind under certain circumstances. Actually it is the same time both inside and outside prison, so you have to gear your mind to working hard and looking forward to starting work the next morning, and perhaps keeping a small diary at night of life in prison with a view to possibly selling it to a newspaper or magazine when you get out, it will all help time to pass quickly.

I realise, as you say, that the conversation might be at a very low ebb, but that in itself is worth observing and recording as a life experience which going to a school would not teach you.

I hope your father is in touch with you regularly.

You have never told me what your feelings were about taking the baby, I would love to talk to you about it sometime. As a person who is interested in lame dogs (being one myself), if you find out what the problem is you can often find a cure, or at least a crutch to help the person along.

Let me tell you that the weather on the outside of prison is just as bloody awful as it is on the inside at the moment.

I am at present trying to write a Fairy Story for children in longhand and finding it very difficult not to make mistakes, but I like a challenge.

I have not any more news to convey to you, so keep your chin up girl, the world is a bloody awful place – it always will be, and as long as you approach it with that in mind, you don't get so many disappointments.

Love, Light and Peace,

SPIKE MILLIGAN

P.S. If there is anything I can send you please let me know, like books, newspapers, or a man.

29th September 1972

My Dear Pauline

Thank you for your letter. I really don't understand this stupid idea of not letting you see all your mail properly. I cannot see what possible harm can be done by a person receiving a letter. I used to think Her Majesty's mail was inviolate. What it means is that it is a breach of privilege and privacy to which I would never subscribe even if I belonged to the police. I hope that this letter is being read by you and not by a policeman.

I don't suppose that at this stage the campaign to try and get you out before time will bear fruit, primarily because the creature called homo sapiens, of which the Home Secretary is one, is completely immovable when it comes to considering human patterns on a psychiatric level. What I mean is if the Home Secretary has never suffered mental stress which has caused mental breakdown he just does not understand the language of the person, who is, in this case, you. I have just managed to get a girl away from two monstrous psychiatrists at Guys Hospital, who had driven her to the stage where she was going to commit suicide. Fortunately, I got her out and passed her into the hands of a human being and now she is safe. So don't expect the world to be a better or worse place when you come out. Nothing has changed – nothing will ever change because man is unchangeable.

No matter what laws are passed there are always people who will act upon them, witness the ordinary German soldier who was told to shoot Jews, women and children as well, and did it because it was the law.

Where are you going when you come out of prison? Are you going to stay with your father? Don't forget I would like to see you once or twice when you get out. Please remember no matter what the conditions are in prison or what they make you do, it is not a permanency, it is going to end shortly, and with that in mind try and take whatever they give you with a degree of rationality, after all, you are an intelligent girl and I think that it is within your means to do it. I agree, passing in a pyjama factory must be soul destroying, but as I say, remember it is coming to an end.

I am sending you a copy of my book of poems called Small Dreams of a Scorpion. I am enclosing an envelope for its return, that is if the prison authorities won't let you have it. I am asking them to return it to me at once and I will keep it for you until you come out. I am sending the book care of the Prison Governor as I don't want it to get lost. I am asking him either to give it to you or send it me back, nothing between will do.

I am flying to Australia to see my mother and brother in a few days time. I will be

away for a month. If you write to me care of
my office they will forward any letters to
me.

Love, light and peace,

SPIKE MILLIGAN

(From the book *The Spike Milligan Letters*, 1977)

ERIC SYKES

Eric Sykes, writer, actor, comedian and golfer knew Spike for more than 40 years, working with him on countless projects and sharing offices, a sense of humour and an agent with him for most of their careers. They were so close, in fact, that some people thought they were interchangeable!

The first time I ever saw Spike was just after I heard his show 'The Crazy People' on the radio when I was in hospital in 1952. It was the best, funniest thing I had ever heard and before I went in for my operation, I wrote a long letter to Spike and his co-writer, Larry Stephens, telling them that. The next day, while I was still sedated after the op., they both popped their heads round my door in the hospital to say hello. The nurse threw them out.

The reason why Spike and I became so close early in our careers is because we both understood the medium in which we were working. At the time it was radio – later we both had to learn how to make the most of movies and TV and we're still learning, still working, still bursting with ideas.

With radio, though, you can use sound and dialogue to paint powerful mind pictures for the listener and Spike did this brilliantly. He painted wonderful pictures with his 'Goon Show' scripts. He used a controlled lunacy. You can't just have lunacy for lunacy's sake. Spike always had a twisted logic running through the 'Goon Show' plots which had its basis in human nature. Greed, cowardice, patriotism, heroism, stupidity, naievete were all there in Grytpype-Thin, Moriarty, Neddy Seagoon, Bluebottle, Eccles, etc. Spike, of course, didn't analyse what he was writing like that. He just wrote things that he knew were funny.

I helped him with some 'Goon Show' scripts when he was under real pressure, trying to imitate the style he created, and we had a huge argument one day over one word which I thought had a fluidity and rhythm. He didn't agree and ended up throwing a heavy paperweight at me. It missed my head by inches, sailing straight out the window and smashing into a million pieces on the pavement three floors below. He's a perfectionist, you see!

I remember Spike had a scene in a film shot at Shepperton. I used to live near there and he spent the night at my house. He was upstairs all evening learning his part then the door to my room burst open and Spike was standing there saying, 'The car is round the front, sir' in an Irish accent.

'That's your line is it?' I guessed.

'Yeah, what d'you think?'

'Does the script call for an Irish accent?'

'No, but I thought . . .

'Just do it normally, then.'

'Normal speaking?'

'Yup.'

'And that's what he did. He came back the next day saying it had all gone really well. When we saw the final film, his scene had been cut.

We've been mates for so long that some people get us mixed up. I was out for lunch with another old pal, Sean Connery, and we were saying goodbye on the street corner when this guy walked up with a glint of recognition in his eye. I stepped back to let him say hello to Sean – famous actor – but he started pumping my hand and saying, 'Fantastic! You're a brilliant writer! I never missed your shows! Such talent!' I was flattered until he walked off muttering, 'Who'd have thought it? Spike Milligan!'

We may both be grey now, but the big difference between me and Spike, of course, is that I walk like a 30-year-old athlete and Spike walks like he's pulling Cyril Smith in a rickshaw. I hope I die before Spike, though. I couldn't bear going to the memorial service and having to sit through Harry Secombe singing 'Bread of Heaven'.

NED'S ATOMIC DUSTBIN

BILL   This is the BBC Light Programme. To add seasonal cheer to the broadcast I have had written permission to wear a small holly leaf in my button hole.

SEAGOON   Don't you realise Wal boy, that the Druids used the holly leaf for certain unsavoury ritualistic rites.

BILL   Oh dear, well I'd better hurry up and get that word cleared by the BBC censorship department. Gid up there!

Grams   Horse gallop off very fast.

F.X.   Knock on door.

HARRY   (*Older than God*) Ahhh . . . mara . . . ahh comeeee . . . ahhhhh . . . ahhhahhhhhhh

MINNIE   He's trying to say 'come in'.

CRUN   Male hormones forever! Ahhh . . .
          hha (*collapses*) Ahhhhh . . . mr . . .

**F.X.   Thud of body and bits of body
          scattering, ball bearings marbles roll
          along floor. Hand full of forks.
          Metallic resonant nuts and bolts
          falling.**

CRUN   Oh dear, he's disintegrated Min . . .
          I'll have to take over his trousers.

**F.X.   Door opens galloping hooves at great
          speed (coconut shells).**

BILL   Ahoy . . . I've come to get clearance
          on a word.

CRUN   What is the word, Sir?

BILL   Well, it's er um . . . um. Yes . . .
          'Holly'!

CRUN   What's wrong with it, Sir?

BILL   Well, it is believed to have
          undertones of eroticism.

CRUN   Oh Dear . . .

MINNIE   Ohhh.

CRUN   Could you write this word down?

MINNIE   Blindfold yourself Henery, don't look!

BILL   Yes . . . I could.

F.X.   Writing.

Grams   Loud startled cluck of chicken . . .

CRUN   (*aside*) Blast! He can write on chickens. You want us to see if this word is fit to be said?

BILL   I fear so.

CRUN   Ohh, well that puts us in rather a nasty spot doesn't it. We don't like committing ourselves.

BILL   But you're the Censors.

CRUN   Ah, but we don't like that sort of thing. We don't do it.

HARRY   (*Yorkshire*) Mr Lord Scradds, you're the oldest, what do you think of this word.

LORD SCRADDS   Ahhhhhhhh . . . ahhh, ahh I'll I won't commit myself at this ahhhhhhhhhhhh at this stage . . . I . . . I'll . . . go along yes . . . I . . . I'll go along . . .

CRUN   Who will you go along with?

SPIKE   Ahhhhhh, anybody a . . .

PETER   (*Aussie*) I think I'm with you there, I'm with you all the way, I'll go along with that.

SPIKE   (*Hooray*) I ratar mark the omplication the most of the marn ave bwin time waste and non the far the plo Car there at Dawn.

CRUN   Ha, ha, ha you devil . . . you devil . . . So then it's agreed that we all agree? Now what was the question?

BILL   The word 'holly', is it –?

MINNIE   Canteen's open!

Omnes   **Scream's of 'Teaaaaaa'**

Grams   **Great rush of boots departing. Distant slamming doors very fast . . .**

SEAGOON   Well, well, well they've escaped under cover of stupidity. Forward Tar Plee ti Pinggeee.

PETER   It is I, Tom.

SEAGOON   Yes it's old 'it is I Tom', Peter Sellers, playboy of Finchley tube station and friend of West End managements.

PETER   I see a vision, Tom.

SEAGOON   Well, hold this song and accompany this next announcement.

PETER   (*Sings idiot tunes behind Bill*)

BILL   Ladies and Gentlemen, what kind of Christmas has it been. Let us recount one, two, three. (*fade*)

Grams   Eccles singing 'Good King Wenceslas' (the choral one).

SPIKE   Hello, Terry Frulls here and we're going over now to the Services Station in the Christmas Islands, over to them.

Grams   Atom bomb . . .

HARRY   (*kid*) Look Mum, another Atom Bomb.

PETER   (*mum*) You lucky boy, that means Daddy will be home early from work.

SEAGOON   Here in London we interview passers by . . . Excuse me, sir, do you believe in a White Christmas?

RAY   Are you kidding?

SEAGOON   Ha, ha, ha and . . . and you, madam, do you believe in an old-fashioned Christmas by the fire?

PETER   (*whoops dear*) Oh, not harf dear.

SEAGOON   Conks? Play that arrangement for nose and harmonica, me? I'm for the old brandy there.

Grams	**Great rush of receding boots . . .**
Max &	**Music**
orchestra	
	(*applause*)
BILL	Tar tar . . . Thank you. Now over Christmas a great story broke, being no newspapers it missed the headlines, but here it is in all it's monkey para toot toot pin pon pee pee peee, tiddley. I doe too is the story of the Tun tack tock!
Orchestra	**Dramatic chords . . .**
SPIKE	It is Christmas and somewhere in a goatskin flat in a naughty Wales, a young hairy titch is working on a painting of a painting!
SEAGOON	(*fade in*) (*sings*) I painted here, I I I I I painted here ha ha ha, now a dab of red here and a touch of puce, here.
CYNTHIA FRUIT	Ohhhh!
SEAGOON	Steady Miss Fruit, keep still . . .
CYNTHIA FRUIT	It's awfully cold posing like this.
SEAGOON	I've got a candle on! Now there! There we are you can relax. It's a master-piece.
CYNTHIA FRUIT	What is it?

SEAGOON   The plans of a new British dustbin.

CYNTHIA FRUIT   And you've had me posing nude for that?

SEAGOON   It's something to do with my unhappy childhood. Off you go and change behind that screen . . . ah! There she goes, TV was never like this . . . Knok, knack knack knock knockitty knock knock knock . . . It's an impression of a door-knocker. Come in!

CRUN   Impression of Innn.

SEAGOON   Steaming Pud, it's me old wrinkled retainer Uncle Crun in his new King-size nightshirt.

Grams   **Whoosh of wind**

CRUN   Ohhhhhhhhhhh!

SEAGOON   I wonder where that draught's coming from.

CRUN   I don't know where it's coming from but I know where it's going. Ah ah ah ah ah Christmas Cracker Joker!

Grams   **Whoosh of wind again (as before)** . . .

CRUN   Ohhhhhhhhhhhh . . . this nightshirt is too big for me, the wind is . . .

SEAGOON   Wait, there's another pair of legs sticking out of the bottom.

CRUN   Ohhhh, who's that in there, come out or I'll . . .

ECCLES   No, I'll come out! 'Ello Neddie, 'Ello Uncle Crun . . . 'Ello, I been slummin.

SEAGOON   Eccles, what you doing in that nightshirt?

ECCLES   Nuttin'. Everything's marked 'Don't touch'.

CRUN   Antiques, you know. But how did you get in? That's what I wanted to know.

ECCLES   I got a map of your legs.

SEAGOON   Come on out at once.

F.X.   **Door opens**

SEAGOON   A door in the nightshirt opened and out stepped a street with a man in it.

GRYTPYPE-
THYNNE   I say, what is all this noise? There's people in that nightshirt trying to sleep you know.

SEAGOON   What, what, what . . . you'll get a biff on the knee. Explain that Krutty hand operated mattress.

GRYTPYPE-THYNNE	That mattress, Sir, contains the princely string and nut-bound body of such stuff as steams are made of, none other than the Count Jim 'Wakey, Wakey' ...
F.X.	**Colossal slap on bare skin (slap stick)**
GRYTPYPE-THYNNE	Stop that revolting scratching will you, Count. The dear Count is plagued this year with a return of the Royal strains.
SEAGOON	Does he really own that nightshirt?
GRYTPYPE-THYNNE	Yes, 'een now, see how he walks the battlements ... Of course he only rents the top.
SEAGOON	What about the rents in the bottom?
GRYTPYPE-THYNNE	Ned, old jokes will get you nowhere. Look what it did to the Count.
SEAGOON	Oh, I apologise for my altitude.
GRYTPYPE-THYNNE	It is low, Ned. Could we sell you an extra three feet?
SEAGOON	Just what I need.
GRYTPYPE-THYNNE	Moriarty, saw three feet off your wooden leg.

MORIARTY	No, I'm going to the ball as a toffee apple.
GRYTPYPE-THYNNE	It's for money!
F.X.	**Furious sawing. End drops off.**
GRYTPYPE-THYNNE	There Ned, three feet.
F.X.	**Till.**
SEAGOON	Thank you. I'll tie it to my head and put a hat on it.
MORIARTY	Ohhh Sapristi! He looks like . . .
GRYTPYPE-THYNNE	Don't tell him!
SEAGOON	Now I must get my plans of the dustbin up to London. Where's the nearest station?
GRYTPYPE-THYNNE	In this cupboard. Admission 3d.
F.X.	**Till. Cupboard door opens.**
Grams	**Station.**
WILLIUM	'Ere shut that door wil yer . . . you want me to catch cold?
SEAGOON	When's the next one to London town devine?
WILLIUM	Arsk that hairy doggie over der.

SEAGOON   Does he speak?

WILLIUM   Does he what? Does he speak? – 'ere listen, listen to this. 'Ello dog, 'ello doggie, go on tell 'im doggie . . . No, he don't speak.

SEAGOON   How does he know when the train goes?

WILLIUM   I told 'im. Ohh! I can I feel a low stabbin' pain in the seams of me underpants. That means it's 9.20! Time to go in it . . . Hold tight.

F.X.   **Guards whistle.**

Grams   **Train whistle. Then horse slowly clops away.**

SEAGOON   Bit short of coal aren't you?

WILLIUM   Yer, you ain't got a bit on you 'ave you?

SEAGOON   No, I gave up carrying it.

WILLIUM   Cor, taking chances eh?

BILL   On arrival in London town devine, Neddie rushed to 10 Downing Street.

F.X.   **Knock on door. Door opens.**

RAY   (*African chief*) What you want man?

SEAGOON   Here, who are you?

RAY   I'm the Foreign Secretary, man.

SEAGOON   Yes, you do look a bit foreign.

RAY   Oh, steady man, that could mean war with Ghana.

PRIME   I say, Brazil, who is that man
MINISTER   blotting out the sun with his head?

RAY   It's a man with a wooden leg tied to his nut with a hat on top.

PRIME   Oh that'll be Lord Hailsham, I
MINISTER   expect.

SEAGOON   No sir, I'm Ned Seagoon. I've got plans.

PRIME   Eh? Let's have a look.
MINISTER

F.X.   **Unrolling plans.**

PRIME   Nothing here.
MINISTER

SEAGOON   The drawings on the other side.

PRIME   Oh, that's a clever idea, who'd have
MINISTER   guessed? Ahhhhh live and learn . . .
plans of new anti-atomic dustbin . . .
Ohhh.

SEAGOON   Yes, you see, in event of radiation,
this dustbin will keep your garbage
atom free.

PRIME   What rubbish!
MINISTER

SEAGOON Indeed.

PRIME MINISTER Well, here's a CBE on account. Now would you like to try for a Knight-star and Garter?

SEAGOON If it's OK with you, sir, it's alright with me.

PRIME MINISTER Good. Come back tomorrow with Hughie Green. Until then a sailor's farewell.

Grams Splash.

F.X. Door slams.
I say, what an ideal intro for Rain Elungton.

Ray Ellington Music quartet
(*applause*)

BILL Hardly had that music ceased and the wind gone up the chimney, when the Prime Minister presented the new atom proof dustbin to a meeting of high-ranking idiots.

Grams Sheep.

PRIME MINISTER Gentlemen, this dustbin has great potential, potontial and puntuntial.

FRED Can it go to the moon?

PRIME MINISTER No, but from small beginnings, y'know, what, what.

MONTY   Is this the prototype?

PRIME   No, that is the dustbin.
MINISTER

F.X.   **Lid of bin lifted up and down.**

MONTY   It sounds like a dustbin.

F.X.   **Dustbin.**

PRIME   (*sudden boyish interest*) I say, may I
MINISTER   try that?

F.X.   **Dustbin sound a little more eager.**

PRIME   Ha ha ha – I say it's not difficult at
MINISTER   all, is it?

F.X.   **Dustbin as above.**

HARRY   (*ageing*) Let . . . I say fellas . . . let me
try now.

F.X.   **Dustbin different tempo to denote
someone else has taken over.**

HARRY   (*ageing*) Oh ha ha ha oh dear, oh
dear, why didn't we get one of these
before, eh?

PRIME   Now me again.
MINISTER

F.X.   **Dustbin.**

Omnes   **All laugh, excited noises about
banging the bin.**

F.X.	**Add dustbins to the above laughter.** (*the above extended*)
PRIME MINISTER	Yes, ahem, now Lord Stron, tell the House of your plan.
LORD STRON	Yes, we intend to find if it's possible for a man to go over the Niagra Falls in this dustbin. (*Cries of here, here*) We've got to keep it pretty dark, otherwise the Russians will start putting dustbins into orbit on the Volga rapids. Gentlemen, if you'll all step into this train . . .
F.X.	**Sound of iron bar clanging.**
BILL	Believe it or not, that was the sound of the Kremlin.
SPOTTOVITCH	Comrade Spondervitch, there is a man outside to see you.
SPONDOVITCH	Comrade Toolsvitch, send him in.
TOOLSVITCH	Come in, son of Mata Hari.
F.X.	**Door opens.**
Grams	**Series of fast approaching footsteps.**
BLUEBOTTLE	The Black Eagle is sitting on the Red Flower Pot.
TOOLSVITCH	The Password!

BLUEBOTTLE	Oh? All is well. Comrades Bluebottleski is here with cardboard to spare.
SPOTTOVITCH	Tell us, comrade what kind of undercover work have you done?
BLUEBOTTLE	(*naughty*) Ohh, I cannot tell that. Oh, I don't know though. Well, I was look-out for the Finchley Wolf Cubs.
TOOLSVITCH	(*keen*) Ahh, what did you spot?
BLUEBOTTLE	I spotted Mrs Evans and the Milkman.
TOOLSVITCH	What did you get for that?
BLUEBOTTLE	A clout on my ear 'ole.
TOOLSVITCH	There is a tin rouble, get the plans of the British anti-atomic dustbin . . . or you will lose your deposits.
ECCLES	What's goin' on here?
TOOLSVITCH	Who are you?
ECCLES	Stalin.
F.X.	**Pistol shot.**
ECCLES	Owwww!
BLUEBOTTLE	You twit, Ecclesavitch. Come wid me . . . farewell comrades. Nothing

but death can stop Bottleski from stealing the plans. Farewell.

F.X. **Door slams . . . door opens.**

BLUEBOTTLE Here, dere's a big spider out dere, Oh!

ECCLES I ain't frightened of big spiders. I'll fix him.

F.X. **Door slams.**

Grams **Terrible battle, Eccles yelling for help. Thuds, bangs etc. Great roaring of a lion aroused.**

F.X. **Door slams.**

BLUEBOTTLE 'Ere where's all your clothes?

ECCLES Bottle, say after me, I must learn the difference between a lion and a spider.

BLUEBOTTLE Ohh . . . ah ha.

Orchestra **Dramatic link.**

SEAGOON Hello folks, Neddie here folks; meantime the plans went ahead to test my dustbin over the Niagra falls. For this the government brought the Niagra Falls to London and put it up at the Savoy. In charge was a master of nuclear explosions.

Orchestra **Last part of the Bloodnok theme.**

Grams	**Bombs exploding etc.**
BLOODNOK	Ohhhhhhh. It's a good job the room's sound proof, poor Frank Sinatra upstairs, my goodness.
Grams	**Atom bomb.**
BLOODNOK	Oh, that was the best explosion of the series.
SEAGOON	Was it Christmas Island?
BLOODNOK	No, Christmas pudding.
SEAGOON	Oh, grand news. We have managed to send an elephant up the Falls in the atomic proof dustbin and it lived.
BLOODNOK	What? No other dustbin has done it and lived.
SEAGOON	Now, next we want a human being to go in it.
BLOODNOK	We'll draw lots for it now. Eccles write your name on fifty pieces of paper, and put them in a hat.
ECCLES	Right, dere.
BLOODNOK	Now, draw it out. What's it say?
ECCLES	Mrs Gladys Smith.
BLOODNOK	You imposter . . . you're not Mrs Gladys Smith, I am!
ECCLES	I don't want to die.

BLOODNOK	You don't want to die you superstitious fool, you superstitious mule you . . . You won't die Eccles. Roll up your trousers!
Grams	Wooden slat blind pulled up.
BLOODNOK	Ohhhhh . . . just as I thought, legs that reach the ground. Now strap him in that dustbin for the test.
ECCLES	No, no let me go! Take your filthy hand off my filthy arm I . . .
Orchestra	Dramatic chords.
Grams	John Snagge: This is London calling in the uncut bicycle service of the Ba Be See. This afternoon the prime minister told an eager half-empty house that today, England would launch an atomic dustbin into the Niagra falls, with a highly qualified pilot at the controls. There were demonstrations at the dustbin launching base, when a million barber electricians carrying soup tureens laid down in the road, with socks full of grit. The driver of the steam roller said 'It was so tempting I'm sorry, I won't do it again' . . . Arsenal 8 – Tottenham 87 . . . (*fade*)
GRYTPYPE-THYNNE	Here that Neddie? They're debasing the use of your original dustbin.

SEAGOON   I'll get my revenge.

MORIARTY   No I'll get mine.

SEAGOON   No no no, thank you, but my revenge is stronger and it lasts the whole drink through.

GRYTPYPE-
THYNNE   Ned, for no reason at all, I will become your solicitor. Take a letter on uncut lino. 'Dear Bloodnok.

F.X.   **Nailing down lino. Continues under dictation.**

GRYTPYPE-
THYNNE   'Unless you return the plans of Ned's dustbin, I will be forced to charge my client a higher rate.' Signed Thynne. Now let me hear that back.

Grams   **Thynne: 'Signed Thynne' played a little faster.**

GRYTPYPE-
THYNNE   Splendid. Now go and lay that under his military kippers.

SEAGOON   Ha ha ha, he who laffs liffs loofs las, ahem, he who har bees, laffs loose lifs. Hee farewell.

Grams   **Whoosh.**

SEAGOON   Bloodnok!

BLOODNOK   Ohhhhhh!

SEAGOON   Ha! Ha! This lino means curtains for you.

BLOODNOK	Lino curtains? What a quaint seasonal custom . . . wait, this is solicitors' lino. You'll hear from my linoleum layer in the morning, Sir. Meantime, take that!
Grams	**Jelly sploosh.**
SEAGOON	What is it?
BLOODNOK	I don't know, Sir. It was dark when I trod in it.
SEAGOON	Gad, it's a banner with a strange device, and clutched by a lad in snow and ice.
BLUEBOTTLE	Get your hands up.
SEAGOON	Bluebottle, take that silly rice-paper off.
BLUEBOTTLE	You touch one hair of dat and Sflaishiou! The disintergarator ray gun will speak in my hand, ha ha ha!
F.X.	**Clang.**
BLUEBOTTLE	Oh, the 'lastic's come off the trigger.
SEAGOON	Don't cry, Bottle, here, have the suspender off my sock.
BLUEBOTTLE	Oh, thanks . . . no . . . no! That suspender is just a glittering Western prize to make me forget my mission. Now, Seagoon, look into my eyes,

toot toot toot . . . little daggers come out and point all the way along my eyes to his, toot toot toot . . . the secrets of Bottle's mesmerism is bending Ned to my will . . . strainnnnnn strainnnnnnn power of eyes, power of eyes . . . Ohhh squint, squint, squint, squinteee . . . Squin . . . ohh, my nose has started to bleed.

SEAGOON   You've crossed your eyes, you nit . . .

BLUEBOTTLE   Oh, no! Den I'm finished with Russia, I am . . . I can't go out wid birds when my eyes are closed.

SEAGOON   We've no time to lose.

BLUEBOTTLE   We must save Eccles from a death worse than fate.

SEAGOON   Yes, we must save Eccles.

BLOODNOK   Ah, but they never did . . . oh dear . . . to think you poor people came all this way for that! Diddle diddle dum . . . well, well, where are the pay offs of yesteryear?

Orchestra   **'Old Comrades March' playout.**

(Goon Show 251 first broadcast on 5 January 1959)

POETRY

BRAVE NEW WORLD

Twinkle Twinkle, little star
How I wonder what you are
Up above the sky so high
Like a diamond in the sky
Twinkle Twinkle, little star
I've just found out what you are
A lump of rusting rocket case
A rubbish tip – in outer space.

(From the book *The Bedside Milligan*, 1971)

THE YOUNG SOLDIERS

Why are they lying in some distant land
Why did they go, did they understand?
Young men they were
Young men they stay
But why did we send them away, away?

(Written during Korean War, 30 March 1955)

MYXOMATOSIS

A baby rabbit
With eyes full of pus
Is the work of scientific us.

(From the book *Small Dreams Of A Scorpion, 1972)*

THE REFEREE
(A brief recountment)

Hannigan's dad was a boxing referee, he referred boxing matches. The fact that he was a confirmed alcoholic produced some startling decisions.

'MacFunn is the winner,' he announced, pointing to a broken, unconscious figure on the canvas.

All hell broke loose, the ring erupted in a sea of flailing managers and seconds. 'What the hell do you think you're doing?' howled the loser's manager.

'Now then,' cautioned Hannigan's Dad. 'Your man lost on a foul, MacFunn was sneezing when he got hit,' so saying he fell down under the weight of alcohol.

There was the Dick Panther versus Killer Blinn affair. The first round was murder. Blinn was hit thirty seven hundred times, six of these by Hannigan's dad. As the gong sounded for the end of the round, Hannigan's dad shouted 'fight on', and insisted on twelve more seconds of fight.

'Injury time,' he announced. An apple core bounced off his head. 'The Queen,' he shouted, stood to attention and fell sideways like a felled ox.

Despite this, he worked regularly in third rate halls, mainly because he was third rate. However, he started to gain a particular notoriety, whereas at one time, bets were on the pugs, betting was now transferred to Hannigan's dad, as to what kind of decision he would make. It got so that people just waited for the end of the bout for the real fun to start. His popularity shot up to a peak when, one night, he disqualified both contestants and declared himself the winner.

Boxing Czar Zoltzman saw a chance to use him.

'Stake him a thousand nicker to tell us who's going to get the decision.'

Hannigan's dad perused the pile of one pound notes on Zoltzman's desk. 'O.K.,' he said, 'Nikky Lewis is going to win in the heavyweight contest.'

At the fight, Hannigan's dad was found in the bar. Never had he had so much drink. Two men carried him into the arena on a stretcher, tumultuous applause greeted him, the boxers entered in comparative silence. While consulting the time keeper, Hannigan's dad fell through the ropes; reaching out to save himself, he inadvertantly pulled the bell cord. Out came the two boxers and set to in their dressing gowns.

'Whoa back,' shouted Hannigan's dad, reappearing. He beckoned the men to the centre of the ring, pulled their heads down, produced a cigar. 'Either of you bums got a light?' he said reeling with laughter.

The first round was noticeable for Hannigan's dad

circling the boxers and singing 'In My Dear Little Alice Blue Gown.' The crowd was only too eager to join in.

Round two saw him staggering dangerously near the fighters. Kerthungggg! a great loping right from Nikky Lewis sent Hannigan's dad staggering, he seemed to go down, but no! shaking his head he flayed into the amazed pugs and sent Nikky Lewis unconscious to the canvas, only to be caught in turn by the remaining, now infuriated boxer.

Down went Hannigan's dad. He stayed down. He died. 'Alcoholic poisoning' was the Coroner's verdict. The strangest verdict to any fight.

(From the book *A Dustbin of Milligan*, 1971)

JOHNNY SPEIGHT

Johnny Speight was an up-and-coming comedy writer when he eventually bumped into Spike in his office above a greengrocer's shop in Shepherds Bush. They went on to make 'Curry And Chips' together for London Weekend Television. One series went out before the IBA slapped a ban on it, saying it was racist. Johnny Speight feels they missed the point.

I first came into business through a friend of mine in the Army. He found out I wanted to get into comedy and put me in touch with Frankie Howerd ... who then put me in touch with Spike and Eric Sykes at their office above Al's Greengrocers in Shepherds Bush. It was in the early 1950s and the 'Goon Show' was already on.

I was overawed by Spike. He was a famous person – a great comic genius – and I was just a bum from Canning Town. But they had read some of my scripts and said they showed promise and they were willing to handle my career.

Eventually, I wrote 'Curry and Chips' which featured Packy Paddy. It was London Weekend Television's first year, but only six shows went out. The IBA made LWT take it off, saying it was racist.

But the coloured people loved it – it was the English who were made to look bigoted in the show, but the people at the IBA could not understand that.

Spike is truthful and funny – he doesn't mind kicking people up the arse. It was marvellous working with him. It was a pleasure having him on the show – and you can't go far wrong with Spike and Eric Sykes in the cast.

Spike has had a tremendous influence on British comedy. Monty Python and the Cambridge Footlights copied him. Everything is derived from something of his – it's almost idolatry.

He has integrity, honesty . . . and talent. He's irreverent and can be offensive – in fact he does it a lot, but he's a breath of fresh air. He's a great innovator and should be on all the time, but people in this country look on comedy as the lowest form of art. In fact, it's the best. It exposes its targets best.

MY COURT MARTIAL

The following is just a thought. I recall the incident from my old Army days. In 1917 the British invented the military tank. Under conditions of great secrecy an attack on the German lines was prepared at Cambrai.

The day before the attack, however, to the amazement of all, the Germans attacked the British with tanks. Immediately a member of the House of Commons demanded an inquiry into our security methods.

> **First day of the inquiry before Lords Blimley, Grumper, and Chattshaw-Blurtington.**

MR SMITH, KC   Lord Spike, you are a General in the British Army?

LORD SPIKE   Ermm, yes.

SMITH, KC   You consider that a living wage?

LORD SPIKE   Errmm. Well, errr –

SMITH   You are living . . .?

LORD SPIKE   Yes.

SMITH   Then you must be getting a living wage.
(*laughter*)

SMITH   Lord Spike, you knew of the promised British tank attack three days before it happened?

SPIKE   Yes, I had been told by the Minister of War.

SMITH   You told no one else?

SPIKE   No.

SMITH   Lord Spike, what I am to reveal to the court may displease you, but reveal it I must. I have here before me a receipt addressed to you from the German Army. It says: 'For services rendered, 10,000 Deutchesmarks.'

SPIKE   I fail to see why the revelation should displease me.

SMITH   For what reason do you receive these payments from the German Army?

SPIKE   I happen to be a Director: have been for several years.

SMITH   I see; in fact you have shares in the German army.

SPIKE   Yes.

SMITH   Lord Spike, is not your loyalty divided between the German and British cause?

SPIKE   Of course not; I serve each office faithfully.

SMITH   Let me amplify your position. Supposing, only supposing, the German Army are building up for an attack on the British. What is your immediate reaction?

SPIKE   As a Director of the German Army it is my duty to keep secret from the British their intention.

SMITH   But you are a General of the British Army. In the light of your knowledge, should you not make defensive preparations?

SPIKE   Of course not. It would ill become my position as a shareholder of the German Army. No sir, when the Germans attacked and only then would I react.

SMITH   You actually mean you are almost Schitzoid in that respect.

SPIKE   Putting it clinically, er – yes.

SMITH   Regarding the tank attack, as the British had only just invented the tank, was it not a great coincidence that the Germans invented it three days before?

SPIKE   It certainly did surprise me – as a British general, that is. Of course as a shareholder in the German Army I knew all the time.

SMITH   Can you explain why three days prior to the British tank attack a telegram was delivered to the General High Command reading 'Build Tanks'?

SPIKE   It was just a coincidence.

SMITH   As the result of a successful German tank attack did not the shares you hold in the German Army increase in value?

SPIKE   Ermmm. Yes.

SMITH   That is all, Lord Spike.

From here on I let the reader take over.

(From the book *A Dustbin of Milligan*, 1971)

SPIKE'S LETTERS

THE DOGSHIT AFFAIR

TO: The Superintendent
Police Station
Harrow Road,
London W2

19th April 1972

Dear Sir,

I want to report an incedint.
*   On Sunday 2nd April, 1972, at*
approximately 4.30 pm. I witnessed two
women and a man with a Great Dane dog – the
dog defecated on the pavement.
*   I followed the people who went to Queens*
Mews.
*   I wrote to the Westminster City Council*

and they told me I should report the
incident to the Police.

As the streets of Bayswater are polluted
excessively by this disgusting habit I do
hope we can prosecute.

Respectfully

SPIKE MILLIGAN

TO: Inspector Haines
Harrow Road Police Station
London W2

16th May 1972

Dear Sir,
Milligan versus Dog Shit
Case Number 2

On Sunday the 7th May at about 11.30 am a
large black dog defecated on the pavement,
I called the creature and said 'Come here
Darling', and saw that its label bore the
address Burnham Court, Moscow Road, and
the dog's name was Liz. A fitting Royal name
for a debasement of the Royal City.

Would you please prosecute?

Sincerely,

SPIKE MILLIGAN

MEMORANDUM

From: Norma Farnes

Copy to: Spike Milligan

Date: 31/5/72

Subject:

INSPECTOR HAINES FROM HARROW ROAD POLICE STATION CALLED IN TO SEE YOU TODAY REGARDING THE LETTER YOU SENT HIM 'MILLIGAN VERSUS DOG SHIT CASE No. 2.'

HE PERSONALLY IS GOING ALONG TO BURNHAM COURT TO SEE THE OWNERS OF THE DOG LIZ. AND GIVE THEM A WARNING. HE SAID HE THOUGHT IT BEST TO GO AND GIVE THEM A WARNING WITHOUT PROSECUTING FIRST BECAUSE YOU WOULD HAVE TO GO TO COURT AND GIVE EVIDENCE, AND HE THOUGHT IT BEST TO GIVE THEM A WARNING. HOWEVER, IF YOU WANT TO PROSECUTE WILL YOU CONTACT HIM.

no don't prosecute – but do warn, What about Dog Shit No. 1?

Memorandum Files Dog X

From: Norma
To: Spike

Date: 23.6.1972

Subject: Inspector Haines from Harrow Road
telephoned regarding Dog Shit No. 1 and Dog
Shit No. 2.

   He has been and warned both of these
people.
   He said what about Dog Shit No. 3!!

      (From the book The Spike Milligan Letters, 1977)

RICHARD LESTER

Richard Lester came to England from America in 1955, just as commercial television started up. He was directing a jazz programme called 'Downbeat' and also got a job coaching young television directors. A gap in the Christmas schedules in 1955 meant that what was essentially a coaching idea went out on prime time television on 23 December. Richard Lester himself described it as a disaster, but it caught the eye of Spike's 'Goon Show' colleague Peter Sellers. TV shows followed and two feature films with Spike – a film of Spike's play 'The Bedsitting Room' and 'The Three Musketeers' – in which Spike was cast as Raquel Welch's husband!

I had a job training young directors for television. We did dummy programmes as part of the course and I did a half-hour of ad-libbed comedy. Round about Christmas, in 1955, there was a hole in the schedules. The powers that be remembered the programme and said 'Do one!' We went on air and it was an absolute total disaster, but because it was sandwiched between the first Christmas panto and Dragnet, we got the fourth highest rating!

I got a telephone call the next morning. A voice said: 'You don't know me, but I saw your programme. Either it was the worst show ever seen on television, or there was something interesting about it.' It was Peter Sellers.

We had lunch to discuss whether a TV version of the 'Goon Show' could be done . . . then went to see Spike.

When I first met him, he was lying on the floor with his head on a coil of thick, hawser rope. He didn't get up and the first thing he said to me was, 'You can't do comedy on TV – there's no point in talking about it.' That was that.

Peter Sellers and I went on with it and we hired Eric Sykes and about 10 writers, including Johnny Speight and Frank Muir. The show, called 'Idiots Weekly Priced Tuppence', was done without Spike or Harry (Secombe).

It was very successfully received. The next day, at 9.30 am, Spike called and said 'I've got the running order for the next show' – and completely took over. Nothing was ever said. We did six programmes and then went on to 'A Show Called Fred' and 'Son of Fred'.

It was madness. There were lots of sets and lots of visual gags. We had to rehearse it during the day and get it out live. It was nightmarish.

But, out of all the people I have known in my life I would rank Spike – along with a couple of others – as having the most extraordinarily inventive mind. I could see him creating when totally unprepared. His work was wonderfully liberating for us, although it wasn't easy. He could be very demanding when he could not produce what he had in mind ... and to do it during one day was almost impossible. With Spike, it was not so much a case of directing, but of creating some order out of much chaos.

I don't see any change in his anarchic qualities of irreverence or a willingness to take on new targets.

He has had THE lasting influence on comedy since the war ... 'The Goons', 'Monty Python', 'Blackadder' ... it's a direct line and you would be hard pressed to find a comedian who would not gladly admit it.'

When Richard Lester made 'The Three Musketeers', he decided to use Spike's services as an actor.

One of the great delights of my career was to cast Spike as Raquel Welch's husband in 'The Three Musketeers'. When I introduced her to the man who was going to be her husband, Raquel had what could only be described as an old fashioned look on her face ... it was a bit of a shock for her!

Spike's first day's work on the film was a scene where he was going to be tortured and interrogated by Charlton Heston. He was very nervous about it, saying 'What am I doing, playing a scene with Charlton Heston – it's such an honour, I can't do it.'

I told him he had to ... and when Charlton came onto the set, HE said: 'I am so much in awe of this – it's so much a privilege to play a scene with Spike Milligan.' That just about sums Spike up.

FIGHT AT ROBIN'S POST IN HAILSHAM

The dance was held in a large and comfortable country-style lounge; chairs and sofas clad in loose floral covers, plenty of polished wood, a few Hercules Brabizon-Brabizon watercolours on walls, standard lamps with few silk shades, a few oriental curios, traces of visits to foreign climes (What are foreign climes? 'Waiter, a pound of foreign climes, please!') As the guests eased themselves in, we were playing lively tunes – 'Woodchoppers Ball', 'Don't Sit Under The Apple Tree', 'Ma, I Miss Your Apple Pie', 'Honeysuckle Rose', 'Undecided', 'Tangerine' (what memories these tunes bring back). Soon the floor was crowded, drinks for the band were arriving at a steady rate. Major Chaterjack, M.C., D.S.O., came over to see that we were being 'looked after'; he was really a great soldier, I for one would have followed him anywhere, preferably away from the war. He was this kind of man. Autumn morning – the early morning had melted the night frost, leaving glistening damp trees. Battery parading – small wafts of steam are appearing from men's mouths and noses – the muster roll is called – B.S.M. is about to report to Major Chaterjack: 'Battery all correct and present, Sir!' The roar of a plane mixed with cannon shells all over the place – M.E. 109 roof top, red propeller boss – Battery as one man into ditch – not Major Chaterjack M.C., D.S.O. – stands alone in the road – unmoved – produces a silver case, lights up a cigarette. He is smoking luxuriously as we all sheepishly rise from what feels like the gutter. He addresses us: 'You realise you did the right thing and I the wrong.' What can you say to a bloke like that?

Interval. We ditch our instruments and wander into the garden for a leak; finding a bush, we 'ease spring'; these were accompanied by the usual postern blasts, each one greeted with cries of 'Good Luck!', 'Fall out the Officers!', 'Drink up! Mine's a Guiness!' As eyes became accustomed to the dark, I was horrified! Five feet from us, on a garden seat, was Lieutenant Goldsmith and a bird. As we slunk away he called out, 'Thank you Gentlemen, and what time is the next performance?' This was too much, we broke out into uncontrollable laughter and once started we couldn't stop. By the time we got to the house I was holding my sides with pain. On entering we saw a huge fat woman, seated at the drums, making a bloody fool of herself. This finished me off. The dance restarted.

Without warning, a Canadian officer poured beer into the bell of my saxophone – (Yes, I also played that) – which he thought funny. I threw the contents on to his jacket, something he didn't think funny. He grabbed the saxophone. I stopped playing. 'Let go,' I said, 'this is a solo instrument.' Our host came over. The Canadian was told that it 'wasn't the done thing.' The dance continued and we, rather I, got drunker. Time now for what I told you was the 'Leg Cocking'; this is an English officer gyration. The man assumes the position for Highland Reel, and then, at the sound of 2/4 or 6/8 tempo, he raises his right leg and leaps all over the room with one hand up in the air and one on his hip. We played 'Highland Laddie'; at once the floor became a mass of leaping twits all yelling 'Och! Aye!' This is where the fighting started. One of the batmen serving drinks had his tray knocked flying all over a Mrs Hendricks. Captain Hendricks hit someone, someone else hit him. This became popular. The room became a melee of fisticuffs and gentlemen. 'Somebody stop them,' shrieked Mrs Hendricks, as someone floored her. Our host rushed up 'Quick, play a waltz.' We launched into 'Moonlight Madonna'. Someone hit Major Chaterjack M.C., D.S.O. His batman laid out the offender, then carried Chaterjack, M.C., D.S.O., to safety. To help it all along, Doug Kidgell threw an occasional cream cake into the arena. The addition of confectionery to the struggling mass made exotic pictures. A red-faced Major, his bald head supporting a cream eclair, hit a Canadian sporting a jam covered ear. Kidgell's masterpiece: a large circular cream-topped cake that stuck to the back of a long officer's head. For moments he stood like Greco's Christ Ascending until a loping right felled him. The cake was picked up by a foot, which trod it all over a chest, that passed it onto a neck. In a short time cream, jam and treacle, were liberally distributed on the uniforms of His Majesty's Officers. Strawberry flan up the front of the jacket, apple strudel on the lower face, plus little blobs of cream on the epaulettes was something we found difficult to salute. Someone covered in lemon-curd was hit backwards through an open window. Our host, his head split open, suddenly appeared rising cross-eyed and smiling above the mass. 'Molly!' he shouted and disappeared again. The news from Moscow was good. Major Chaterjack, M.C., D.S.O. had recovered enough to come on again and was rendered unconscious for a second time. He was immediately trodden underfoot. His batman grabbed his ankles and pulled him from the carnage, a seraphic smile on his face. There seemed no sign of the fight abating, so we played 'God Save The King' and packed our gear.

There was a lot of booze left in the kitchen. We drank it. Legend has it I slid to the floor, first calling for my mother or a priest. To make matters worse, the band truck wouldn't start, so Edgington and Fildes dragged me along between them, with Kidgell walking behind making remarks. The billet was a mile and a half away, but after a while the Gunners Edgington and Fildes dropped Gunner Milligan in a ditch and said 'Sod it.' They sat a while smoking and Driver Kidgell said 'I'll go and phone for a truck.' An hour later the water waggon arrived. It was two in the morning and I was starting to surface enough to notice that all the dragging had removed the soles from my boots. There was only enough room for three in the cabin, so Edgington and I sat astride the water tank on the back and drove through the black silent streets of Hailsham shouting 'Night Soil'. Thank God there wasn't any.

(From the book *Adolf Hitler, My Part In His Downfall*, 1971)

TERRY NATION

Writer Terry Nation terrified the children of Britain in 1963 when the creatures he created trundled across the country's TV screens in 'Dr Who' – 'The Daleks'. He is, perhaps, better known for his science fiction work on 'Dr Who' and 'Blake's Seven' than he is as a comedy writer, but he will forever be in debt to Spike Milligan – to the tune of pounds ten!

Spike Milligan actually gave me my very first break in the business. I had been failing miserably at everything I had been trying to do. I had failed as a stand-up comic, and I got an introduction to meet Spike, and as far as I was concerned, he was a big star. 'The Goon Show' was on and every young person in the country was a 'Goon Show' fan.

I went to meet him, and he chatted for a minute, and then he took a longer look at me and said,

'When did you last eat?' I said, 'Well . . . Thursday,' and this was Wednesday, I suppose. My hair was long, and I was starving to death. He instantly wrote a cheque for ten pounds, and that was a lot of money in those days. He said, 'Go away and write a "Goon Show", and if it's any good, we'll represent you.'

Let me just tell you what representation was. Some other writers, Galton and Simpson were writing 'The Hancock Show' at the time, Eric Sykes was also writing a big show, and together with Spike they had formed this kind of agency, it was a group of artists running their own agency.

I went back to my digs, wrote the episode that night and had it on his desk the next morning. The very next day, he said, 'Okay, we'll represent you', and shortly after that, I got a job on a new show. It was a disaster, but at the end of it, I was a writer.

Milligan is a very generous, warm man, and I would undoubtedly have quit had it not been for his coming up with that opportunity. When people ask me how I got started, I got started because of Spike Milligan.

POETRY

NONESENSE II

Myrtyle milled the Miller pole
While Tommy twigged the twoo
And Dolly dilled the dripper dole
As willy wet the woo
Then Andy ate the Acker-cake
And Wendy wonged the groo
As Herbert hacked the hatter rake
And Bertha bonged the boo!
Then all together honged the hack
And widdle donkey doo
They pongled on the wally wall
And the time was half-past two.

(From the book *The Bedside Milligan*, 1971)

THE SIEGE OF FORT KNIGHT

An underwater military gas stove is all that stands between Fort Knight and annihilation at the hands of the Biguns tribe. But – can Inventor Crun construct one in time? (He can't get the wood, you know.) Can Major Seagoon get it to the fort on time? The journey is fraught with impossibilities. Thus unfolds the gripping saga of a Long March – long by anyone's calendar . . .

WALLACE   For the last time this evening at popular prices, the unpopular face of capitalism – The Goon Show.

Orchestra   **Corny chords**

SEAGOON   Presenting the Siege of Fort Knight.

WALLACE   The scene – a lonely British outpost in a lonely British outpost.

ARMY OFFICER   Gentlemen, as you see on this map, thirty thousand miles away deep in the liver of Africa –

SEAGOON   You mean the heart, sir.

ARMY OFFICER   No! This place is much further down. In the depths of the jungle and despair, the gallant British garrison at Fort Knight are hard pressed by Bigun natives –

SEAGOON   Biguns?

ARMY OFFICER   Yes, some have very big 'uns. Unless this garrison is relieved within **fourteen days**, Fort Knight is finished, and I feel a terrible pun coming.

SEAGOON   Can't they hold out for an extra week?

ARMY OFFICER   Rubbish. Who's heard of a fortnight lasting three weeks?

MATE   I have – it was in Scunthorpe.

ARMY OFFICER   Fort Knight needs relief.

SEAGOON   Reinforcements?

ARMY OFFICER   No, no they all have men they require.

SEAGOON   Ammunition?

ARMY OFFICER   They've plenty!

SEAGOON	Provisions?
ARMY OFFICER	They've got ample.
SEAGOON	They can't live on ample alone.
ARMY OFFICER	Worse, they've got nothing to cook it on.
SEAGOON	Uncooked ample – you know what that means.
MATE	The squits!
SEAGOON	In a matter of days they'll be struck – no laundry will go near them.
ARMY OFFICER	And in forty eight hours the monsoon will arrive.
SEAGOON	Bang in the middle of a rainy season.
ARMY OFFICER	The point is, when it does break –
SEAGOON	Yes, yes, yes, yes, yes, yes?
ARMY OFFICER	I wish you wouldn't do that! When it breaks, the river Dongler will rise and the fort will be under nine feet of – er – what do you call it –
MATE	Water.
SEAGOON	Gad. What's the answer?
ARMY OFFICER	They'll need underwater gas stoves.
SEAGOON	No such thing's been invented.

ARMY OFFICER   Ah, that's only because nobody has made one. But there is one man.

SEAGOON   One? Come on, there's quite a few of us. Ha ha!

ARMY OFFICER   I mean, I know one man who **might** be able to help.

SEAGOON   Not – not – not Dick Scratcher?

ARMY OFFICER   You're dead right – it's not Dick Scratcher. It's Henry Crun – the world's greatest underwater inventor.

Orchestra   **Woeful music**

GRUN   (*sings*) **Around the world in eighty three days, I travelled –**

F.X.   **Knock at door**

MINNIE   I recognise that – it's a knock.

F.X.   **Knocking**

CRUN   Come in.

SEAGOON   Good evening.

MINNIE   Evening.

F.X.   **Door opens and shuts**

CRUN   I can see you beat the door to it. Good evening.

OMNES	EVENING, EVENING, EVENING. (*pause*)
SEAGOON	Good evening.
OMNES	GOOD EVENING, EVENING, EVENING.
CRUN	Are you the elephant man?
SEAGOON	Elephant man? What are you on about?
CRUN	I'm on about £12 a week.
SEAGOON	Listen, I'm from the War Office.
CRUN	War? No thank you, we've just had one!
SEAGOON	I'm here on a mission.
F.X.	**Tambourine and tuba accompaniment**
CRUN AND MINI	(*sing*) Come and join us, come and join us . . .
SEAGOON	Wrong – wrong – wrong mission! Mr Crun –
CRUN	Yes.
SEAGOON	Can you invent a waterproof gas stove for cooking ample?
CRUN	A waterproof gas stove? It's going to be very difficult. You see, you can't get the wood, you know. Can't get it.

SEAGOON   Have you ever built such a thing before?

CRUN   Well, in a manner of speaking – **no**. You can't get the wood, you see.

SEAGOON   Is there no way?

CRUN   Yes definitely, definitely there is! But it will be difficult.

SEAGOON   Why?

CRUN   Because you can't get the wood.

SEAGOON   I can get you the wood.

CRUN   Ah, well that's going to be very difficult.

SEAGOON   Why?

CRUN   I won't be able to go around saying 'You can't get the wood' anymore.

F.X.   **Strange unearthly metallic sound**

SEAGOON   Gracious, what's that?

CRUN   That's Min playing a gas stove.

SEAGOON   Ah! How long would it take you to waterproof one?

CRUN   Well, that depends on how much you'd be willing to pay.

SEAGOON   Thirty thousand pounds!

F.X. **Construction noise at colossal high speed, running footsteps, shouts and yells**

CRUN (*exhausted*) Where's the money?

SEAGOON It is waterproof?

CRUN We'll soon find out.

MINNIE What is it, ducky?

CRUN Min, just get into the gas oven, would you?

F.X. **Door closes**

MINNIE (*echo*) What have you put all these potatoes in with me for, Henry?

CRUN Just in case, Min.

MINNIE (*echo*) In case of what, Henry?

CRUN Yes, in case of what. Mr Seagoon, help me throw this into the river.

F.X. **Splash. Bubbles**

CRUN Min!

MINNIE (*echo*) Yes, Henry?

CRUN Are the potatoes still dry?

MINNIE Yes, Henry.

CRUN Hooray, it's working.

MINNIE That's more than British Leyland.

SEAGOON Brilliant, Mr Crun. I'll order one right away.

CRUN How many ones?

SEAGOON One one.

CRUN One one? Oh dear, it's a lot of work making one one. Couldn't you order **one** one **one** one **one**?

SEAGOON Alright – one, one one one one.

CRUN I just remembered –

SEAGOON What?

CRUN You can't get the wood, you see.

SEAGOON Very well, I'll take the one you just made.

MINNIE (*off*) Helppp!

CRUN Too late, it's drifting away down the stream.

SEAGOON Quick – follow that gas stove –

F.X. **Splash as body enters water**

MINNIE (*distant*) Help! Help! Save me and the potatoes!

SEAGOON (*swimming*) Hold on, Madam . . . (*fade*)

Max and Orchestra **Music**

WALLACE   While Secombe rescued the
            prototype – Min and the potatoes –
            Henry Crun struggled manfully with
            making a second waterproof gas
            stove. Within a month captain
            Seagoon and his gas stoves arrived at
            the base camp in Africa to arrange
            transport with a military band.

Grams   Military brass band music.

BLOODNOK   Ah, Seagoon, bad news – I've got a
            temperature, but I'm going to carry
            on.

SEAGOON   What is your temperature?

BLOODNOK   98.4

SEAGOON   That's normal.

BLOODNOK   I know, that's why I'm carrying on.

SEAGOON   Good, now how are we to get the
            waterproof gas stoves from here to
            the garrison? Helicopter?

BLOODNOK   Impossible, sir, impossible. The fort
            is invisible from the air. And worse
            still – the air is invisible from the
            fort.

SEAGOON   By road, then?

BLOODNOK   No road.

SEAGOON   The river?

BLOODNOK   No.

SEAGOON   Down the river.

BLOODNOK   No.

SEAGOON   Across the river into the trees?

BLOODNOK   No.

SEAGOON   Why not?

BLOODNOK   No trees.

SEAGOON   Across the trees into the river?

BLOODNOK   No river.

SEAGOON   Rail?

BLOODNOK   Doesn't run.

SEAGOON   Why not?

BLOODNOK   No railway.

SEAGOON   Could we build one?

BLOODNOK   The river would wash it away.

SEAGOON   You said there was no river.

BLOODNOK   It's behind the trees.

SEAGOON   A moment ago you said there weren't any trees.

BLOODNOK   Ah, they've grown since then. Time can't stand still for you, you know.

SEAGOON   Wait! I remember seeing an armoured train at the depot.

BLOODNOK   That train was only armoured from the inside.

SEAGOON   Why?

BLOODNOK   We couldn't fire out, but they could fire in.

SEAGOON   Why was that?

BLOODNOK   The windows faced inwards.

SEAGOON   Then we'll use that!

F.X.   **Guard's train whistle. Engine hooter – train puffs out of station**

BLOODNOK   Now, to keep the engine driver alert I've brought me bagpipes.

F.X.   **Bagpipes drone into life**

SEAGOON   Why didn't we think of that before? Meanwhile, at Fort Knight – (*from now on very fast*)

F.X.   **Gunfire, bugles**

SPIKE   Meanwhile, Mr Crun –

CRUN   You can't get the wood, you know.

SEAGOON   Yes! Yes! Meanwhile, back in Fort Knight –

F.X.	**Gunfire, bugles**
SEAGOON	On the armoured train
F.X.	**Trains and bagpipes**
BLOODNOK	We shall have to use electrified Mongolian bagpipes.
SEAGOON	Why didn't we think of that before? Meanwhile, at Fort Knight –
F.X.	**Gunfire, bugles**
SPIKE	While back with Crun –
CRUN	. . . the wood, you know.
SEAGOON	. . . Fort Knight
F.X.	**Gunfire, bugles**
SPIKE	At this very moment in London's West End –
Grams	**Victor Sylvester's 'Come Dancing' music**
SEAGOON	On the armoured train –
F.X.	**Train, bagpipes**
SPIKE	Meantime in Chapter Two!
F.X.	**Phone rings**
BLOODNOK	Hello? Armoured train.
F.X.	**Tom-toms**

NATIVE   (*distorted*) Listen, Bloodnok. This Chief of Biguns Tribe. I give you warning. If you proceed with waterproof gas stove at Fort Knight, we poison the drinking water . . . Ha! Ha! He! He!

BLOODNOK   You over acting swine!

SEAGOON   Keep him on the line.

F.X.   Whoosh

BLOODNOK   Right. Listen, you devil –

NATIVE   (*distorted*) I kill everything in your body, I put spear –

F.X.   Pistol shot

NATIVE   Argghhh!

SEAGOON   (*on phone*) Bloodnok?

BLOODNOK   Yes.

SEAGOON   I've got him!

BLOODNOK   Splendid. Now get back here right away. Crun's just arrived with an improved waterproof gas stove Mark II.

Orchestra   Dramatic chords

WALLACE   Hurrying overland, Crun reached base camp disguised as a bale of tobacco.

SEAGOON	Crun, you've arrived in the nicotine!
F.X.	**Tearing paper wrapper**
CRUN	Look – voila!
SEAGOON	That's not a voila! That's the stove.
CRUN	Yes. I'll just get in and turn on the gas and set the regulo at 3.
F.X.	**Switch**
Grams	**Organ music: Reginald Dixon's 'I do like to be beside the seaside'**
CRUN	(*echo*) Dear, dear, that's not right. I'll try regulo 2. I'll just have a look inside the oven . . .
F.X.	**Door opens**
Grams	**Railway station noises**
TANNOY	The train now standing at Platform 3 . . .
WELSHMAN	Pardon me, but where's the taxi rank?
CRUN	I'm sorry, I'm a stranger round here.
WELSHMAN	Oh! Where do you come from?
CRUN	Africa.
WELSHMAN	Oh. Would you mind closing the oven door, there's a draught in the waiting room?

F.X. **Door closing**

CRUN   Amazing. Let me see. I think I can see what the trouble is. I had the regulo on 5. It should have been on 2. Now let's see what we get.

Quartet **Music**

CRUN   No. there's still something wrong!

SEAGOON   Crun! We can't waste time like this!

CRUN   You know a better way?

SEAGOON   Yes – here it comes. We **must** get to the fort. There's very little time left or right! Bloodnok!

BLOODNOK   He must mean me!

SEAGOON   We must set off imediately.

BLOODNOK   You're dead right. We must do it today, or we'll never get another chance. Eccles, help me get these gas stoves on your head.

ECCLES   Eccles Plenty of room. OK. How far do I have to carry them?

BLOODNOK   A thousand miles.

ECCLES   I got to walk all the way?

BLOODNOK   No. Part of the way you'll be allowed to run.

ECCLES   You bastard! (censored)

SEAGOON	Bloodnok, we have to keep this expedition a closely guarded secret.
BLOODNOK	Don't worry. The camels are all disguised as men.
SEAGOON	And the men?
BLOODNOK	Heavily disguised as camels.
SEAGOON	Were you trained at MI5?
BLOODNOK	As a dustman!
SEAGOON	What a disguise.
Orchestra	**Safari music – dramatic chords**
SEAGOON	Thus began a remarkable march of forty-seven days. Forty-seven days is remarkable for the month of March.
BLOODNOK	To conserve energy we marched lying down and only stood up to sleep.
SEAGOON	Meanwhile at Fort Knight (*silence*)
ECCLES	Early closing!
F.X.	**African drums**
BLOODNOK	That night amid the sound of jungle drums, we were confronted by the Biguns natives, some in warpaint, some more civilized in wallpaper. As we neared the Fort we became familiar with African customs.

AFRICAN   Anything to declare, white man?

BLOODNOK   A waterproof gas stove.

AFRICAN   Ymblum naba Blum. Importation of gas stove you pay three elephant tusks.

BLOODNOK   Where do you expect me, from Catford SE6, to get elephant tusks?

AFRICAN   I sell you.

BLOODNOK   How much?

AFRICAN   One waterproof gas stove.

BLOODNOK   What luck! Eccles give him one of the waterproof gas stoves.

AFRICAN   Here – tusks.

F.X.   **Crashing of tusks**

ECCLES   Oh. Now he's got a waterproof gas stove.

BLOODNOK   What luck. *Just* what we need. I say, tribal fellow, how much you want for waterproof gas stove?

AFRICAN   Three elephant tusks.

BLOODNOK   Three? Just what we've got –

SEAGOON   News from Fort Knight! They've only enough uncooked ample to last another hour.

BLOODNOK Well, it's only eighteen miles as the crow flies, but our crow is sick with lurgi.

SEAGOON Eighteen miles, through native tribes. It means certain death or certain life.

BLOODNOK One of us must volunteer.

SEAGOON Yes, one of us must volunteer.

ECCLES One of us **must** volunteer.

BLOODNOK Good old Eccles.

ECCLES No. Bad old Eccles.

SEAGOON Brave boy Eccles.

ECCLES No, coward Eccles.

SEAGOON You coward.

ECCLES I'm a coward.

BLOODNOK You coward.

ECCLES You coward.

SEAGOON You coward.

BLOODNOK Well, it's no good **three** cowards going.

SEAGOON (*calls*) Mr Crun! Mr Crun, we have one hour in which to cover eighteen miles to the fort. Any suggestions?

CRUN Well, we could go by train. That's regulo 5.

F.X.	**Switch**
SEAGOON	Good. Open the oven door!
F.X.	**Door opens. Sound of trains**
TANNOY	Train now standing at platform 7 of the gas stove, is for Fort Knight.
CRUN	(*echo*) Just in time. Everybody into the gas stove, I'll get in first. Come on. Hand me in the right side of the stove. Now the left. Now the top and the back. Now close the oven door from the outside and bring it in after you.
ECCLES	Wait a minute. Close it on the outside? And bring it in after me? That would mean climbing through it when it's shut and not opening it till I get through.
SEAGOON	Well? What are you waiting for?
ECCLES	I don't know how to do it.
SEAGOON	We'll take the rest of the oven by train. **You** get the oven door and go ahead on foot. Is that all clear?
ECCLES	Er –
SEAGOON	Good. Swallow this road map and follow instructions.
Orchestra	**Dramatic chords**

SEAGOON　Within an hour we were at the gates of Fort Knight.

F.X.　**Gunfire, bugles. Native warriors**

CRUN　I'll ring.

F.X.　**Doorbell**

SEAGOON　I'll do the talking. I've got an 11-plus, you just look intelligent.

ECCLES　Oh, dear.

F.X.　**Door opens**

BUTLER　Was that **you** ringing, sir?

SEAGOON　No, it was the bell. We'd like to speak to the Commanding Officer.

BUTLER　I'll see if he's in, sir.

F.X.　**Door closes**

SEAGOON　He was a nice fellow – I wonder why he was nude.

F.X.　**Door opens**

BUTLER　Pardon me, sir, they're rather busy at the moment. If you could leave your card?

SEAGOON　My card? It's in my other suit.

BUTLER　Perhaps you'd like to stay to tea, sir.

SEAGOON　Oh, that is kind.

BUTLER	You must excuse the confusion, we have enemies of the Queen here.
SEAGOON	Oh, are they stopping here as well?
BUTLER	Yes, it's all very confusing at meal times. Is yours the waterproof gas stove we've been expecting?
SEAGOON	Yes. Could we connect it to the mains?
BUTLER	I'm afraid that would serve no purpose.
SEAGOON	What do you mean?
BUTLER	The gas was cut off yesterday. A matter of a quarter in arrears.
SEAGOON	Never mind. We mustn't fail now. Eccles, open that brown paper parcel.
ECCLES	(*sings as opens parcel*) Oh! It's you!
BLUEBOTTLE	Yes, I've seen the light, Captain. I'm the rescue plan. Hello, everybody. I heard you call.
SEAGOON	I haven't called yet.
BLUEBOTTLE	I'm answering in advance. Strikes answering-in-advance pose, well forward on balls of feet.
SEAGOON	Get into the gas stove and connect this cylinder of gas.

BLUEBOTTLE   Yes, I will, Capatain. I will do that.
Enters gas stove, and assumes
crouching position within, as
assumed by certain people in *Bridge
Over The River Kwai*, playing South
London all next week. Fixes gas
cylinder. Here, I smell gas.

SEAGOON   Can you see where the leak is?

BLUEBOTTLE   No, it's very dark in here.

SEAGOON   Well strike a match.

BLUEBOTTLE   Alright, Captain. Oh, wait a minute.
Are you sure this match will not
ignite the gas, thereby deading me, as
it has on previous occasions?

WALLACE   Listeners, stand by for the obvious.

SEAGOON   Of course not, they're safety
matches.

BLUEBOTTLE   Thank you for your words of
comfort, Captain. I trust you with
my life. I do do that, yes. I will strike
a match now. Strikes safety match
for safety.

F.X.   **Strikes match**

BLUEBOTTLE   Ah-hah! You're waiting for me to get
deaded, aren't you? But I'm not
going to. This week Bluebottle is not
going to be deaded. So there.

F.X.	**Explosion, followed by knock on door. Door opens.**
POSTMAN	Brown paper for you, sir.
ECCLES	Thank you.
F.X.	**Paper being torn off parcel**
ECCLES	Oh – it's you!
BLUEBOTTLE	You rotten swine, you! Seeks among debris for shattered underpants, shredded boots and three 1″ by 1½″ lumps of head.
SEAGOON	But lad, you've done it!
BUTLER	Compliments of the besieged garrison, sir, could you make your explosions quieter? We can't hear ourselves fight.
SEAGOON	Don't you realise, below stairs fool, the underwater gas stove has exploded!
BUTLER	Oh, dear, and I had the Sunday joint all ready. This will mean surrender to the enemies of the Queen.
SEAGOON	Surrender?
BUTLER	Surrender.
BLOODNOK	Surrender?
SEAGOON	To the enemies of the Queen?

BLOODNOK   A splendid idea, I'll put my coward set on!

SEAGOON   No, go in there and fight. Give out the swords. Open the gate and we'll charge.

F.X.   **Door opens**

SEAGOON   Charge! Wait! There's nobody here.

BLOODNOK   They've all gone.

ECCLES   There's not a soul.

SEAGOON   What a disappointing ending to a show.

WALLACE   Perhaps listeners will now believe how bad things really are in the Old Country. Good Night.

(From the Vintage Goon Show 13, recorded 16 March 1958,
first broadcast 27 December 1988)

JOHN BLUTHAL

The Australian actor, John Bluthal, had a long associ-
ation with Spike. Since they first began working
together in Australia, John Bluthal was a stalwart of
Spike's radio and TV shows ... and also starred in
Spike's play, 'The Bedsitting Room'. It was an unusual
recording of the actor's voice that convinced Spike that
he should work with him.

I was in Australia doing a vaudeville series and I
did a radio show 'Three's A Crowd' – with
Michael Bentine. Michael took a tape of 'Three's
A Crowd' over to Spike, who eventually came
over to Australia to record a radio show. I helped
him cast the actors.

Spike mentioned the tape of 'Three's A Crowd'
and said 'I heard it at the wrong speed – you
sounded great so I booked you!'

He's brilliant and I've had some great moments
with him. There were times when he was doing a

show, when he'd call me up and say that he wanted me in it . . . when I was in Australia! He'd just say 'Get on a plane and come straight to the BBC, pick up a script, have a day to look at it and then we'll start.'

He was very helpful when I decided to come to England. When we were doing 'The Bedsitting Room it varied and changed all the time . . . new ideas were always being incorporated. People came to see it over and over again, because it was different every night.

I remember one night, it was St Patrick's Day but Spike had forgotten. While I was off stage at one point, I painted a huge shamrock on my face. I came back on stage and he said, 'You've got a shamrock on your face'.

I said, 'It's St Patrick's Day'. He replied, in an Irish accent, 'Glory to God, so it is' – and we did the rest of the show in Irish accents.

We used to write letters to each other. He sent a picture from a film once and had written, 'What does it feel like to be Jewish and ugly' on it? I sent it back saying, 'Better than being Irish and incurable.' Back it came, with the words; 'I don't wish to know that' on it.

There was another time, when we were doing a sketch – Dr Finlay's Casebook for Uganda. I was the patient and Spike was the doctor. We had to be dressed up as natives and there was no full dress rehearsal. When we did the sketch, Spike looked at me in full gear and started getting terrible giggles during the recording. He was convulsed and could not get a line out.

At the end he explained why – he said 'I looked at you and I suddenly saw a Polish, Jewish, Australian black man, speaking with a Scottish accent – it's the funniest thing I've ever seen'.

POETRY

THE PRAYER OF THE CIVIL SERVANT

When it's OBE time in England
And the knighthoods flow like wine,
In next year's Birthday Honours
If you're stuck for a name, use mine.

Chorus: Rule Britannia, etc., etc.

(From the book *A Book Of Bits Or A Bit of A Book*, 1965)

THE LOONEY

In Kilburn lived a fine wreck of a man, one Mick Looney. At this moment he stood in the corner of a muddy building site that was forever England, spiteful C of E rain was falling on good Catholics. Looney was talking to himself out loud – he was deaf: 'Me farder tole me from der Kings of Catlick Oireland, so why I am I standin' here in der pissin' rain mixin' cement for Mowlems?'

Even now the torrent was turning the cement into viscous watery soup that would one day be a floor that would fall on the roof of the tenants below.

Looney was five feet eight inches, because he hadn't gone metric. Laid on a slab his body would have invited immediate burial; he dared not fall asleep in parks for fear of people calling the Coroner. His body had never seen the sun, or for that matter the moon. Middle-aged, he had a face like a dog's bum with a hat on; two enamel blue eyes stared blankly from a DIY head.

We move now to 113b Ethel Road, a building with a slight tendency to fall down, built in Victorian days in the mock-Gothic style now mocked by everyone. Looney made 'improvements': out came those silly sash windows, in went those Ted Moult ones you 'can't hear helicopters in the garden through'. He assured his wife that 'dis will increase der price of der house', as he planted plastic tulips in the front garden . . . in December.

The building was riddled with rising damp – he had put rat traps down and caught fish. It had deathwatch beetle, dry rot, damp rot – take them away and the building wasn't there. The top floor he had 'converted' to flats, only just better than being converted to Protestantism.

This Sunday the skies above Kilburn hung with pre-natal clouds, pregnant with chilling rain. The wife Mary and son Dick were at mass devoutedly praying, 'Please God let us win Littlewoods, say £500,000'. Looney 'himself' was at home in his best suit, or the best he'd got – he had seen it in Burton's window in 1947 on a Clarke Gable lookalike dummy. When Looney forced his rotund body into it, it took on the appearance of a python that had swallowed a cripple. After fifteen years, his wife had donated it to 'Clothe the Ethiopian Poor' – they had sent it back to him with a pound.

Returning from Mass his family found him slavering over *News of the World* 'POPSTAR'S NUDE NIGHT OF SIN IN TRANSPARENT KILT!' and 'NUDE NEGRO VICAR RUNS AMOK WITH FEATHER DUSTER!' 'PRINCE PHILIP, IS HE A TRANSVES-TITE?'

He greeted his spouse, 'Ah, me darlin', how long will lunch be?'

'It should last about an hour,' she said as she slaved over a raging hell of a black stove with hellish pots issuing boiling vapour.

The food wasn't being cooked so much as tortured. Der British is terrible cooks, thought Looney, they even burnt Joan of Arc. Great jets of steam ascended upwards – after years of this there was now more nourishment in the ceiling than the food.

Looney stood to stretch his legs and collided with the washing line above. Astride his head like a jockey sat his wife's voluminous bloomers, a sexual obstacle – but for them he would have done it many more times. Grabbing the arms of the swollen imitation moquette chair he slowly lowered himself, the huge chair appeared to be devouring him. Down he went until his bum had noisily driven the last of the creaking springs to the floorboards.

He read from the *Exchange and Mart Gazette*:

Wanted, ten gallons of fish oil, will exchange for set of Indian clubs.

Twenty tins of dog food, will exchange for any Vera Lynn records or photo of the Shroud of Turin.

Old style wooden leg, owner going abroad, will sell or exchange for Tupperware set.

'Ah! Here's me advert,' he said and read aloud: 'Wanted, throne like chair, price negotiable o.n.o. or will exchange for house-trained pure-bred mongrel and good barker, aged three but looks older o.n.o.'

RICHARD INGRAMS

Richard Ingrams, the editor of the 'Oldie Magazine' and the former editor of 'Private Eye', first came into contact with Spike Milligan in 1961. Richard Ingrams and John Duncan had set up a theatre company and they wrote to Spike asking if he had a play they could use. Spike sent them one that had been gathering dust . . .

We had a theatre company called 'Tomorrow's Audience' and we'd been given the run of the Marlow Theatre in Canterbury for a couple of weeks. We got in touch with Spike and asked if he had a play. He'd written 'The Bedsitting Room' with John Antrobus and it was just lying at the bottom of a drawer somewhere. He dug it out and sent it to us.

We put it on, but Spike took no interest in it at all . . . until it started getting good reviews. Then he came down to see it and eventually he was in it in the West End. I just don't think he'd thought it was any good until he saw it . . .

I then joined 'Private Eye' full time . . . Spike always took a great interest in the 'Eye'. He was always sending in letters, verses and pictures that he'd captioned with speech bubbles.

I remember when we had our first big libel case – which was the Randolph Churchill case – Spike wrote to us shortly afterwards asking couldn't he be libelled. He'd always wanted to be libelled.

In the next issue I wrote 'Spike Milligan Is A Dirty Irish Poove' – and he sued on the grounds that we'd called him IRISH! We made a token payment as settlement.

Spike also had me in the Q5 series along with John Wells. We were the straight men . . . and Spike always had to have a straight man to play off. I remember there were times when there was a studio audience and Spike would just be shouting at the producer and making jokes about him.

I think a lot of people at the BBC didn't really understand him and thought he was out of control . . . and the BBC never had the producers who could match him. In fact, Spike always had a clear sense of how far he could go, but people used to think that if they had him on, he'd run amok. He's always been fantastically hard-working and he's a true professional. There were been times when he was sitting in his dressing room with his head in his hands, but he still went out and performed.

But he had an enormous influence . . . especially on the Pythons although I never found them as funny as Spike.

His writing is also very funny. I think his best stuff is in the Edward Lear class, but it is never regarded as such.

POEM

PHILIP LE BARR

Philip Le Barr
Was knocked down by a car
On the road to Mandalay
He was knocked down again
By a dust cart in Spain
And again, in Zanzibar

so,

He travelled at night
In the pale moon-light
Away from the traffic's growl
But terrible luck
He was hit by a duck
Driven by – an owl.

ILLNESS IS GOOD FOR YOU

One good appendicitis –
Or a cure for St. Vitus dance
Pays for a Harley Street Surgeon's
Vacation in the South of France.

THE BEDSITTING ROOM

On the first anniversary of the Nuclear Misunderstanding that led to World War III, LORD FORTNUM OF ALAMEIN is visiting CAPTAIN PONTIUS KAK, eminent psychiatrist and dealer in Army surplus, who bids him lie on a couch beneath a feather suspended above his belly button. KAK walks to head of the couch, goes to sit on an empty space. At the last moment a DICKENSIAN CLERK holding a chair under himself slides underneath KAK, so that KAK is seated in his lap. This is all done in one smooth movement.

KAK   Now then, start at the beginning, tell me all.

FORTNUM   My parental ancestor Lord Crapologies Fel de Minge.

KAK   (*Quietly without stopping FORTNUM speaking*) Did he?

FORTNUM   What? Came over with the William The
           Conqueror, first class of course . . . it was
           Hastings Ten Sixty-six . . .

KAK   (*writes down on pad*) Hastings Ten Sixty
           Six. Right, I'll phone him later.

FORTNUM   Yes, he'll bear me out . . . Well, he was a
           tall man with garnished ginger knees and
           several ways about him. On Sundays they
           say he took a spotted woman to church
           . . . Now in the late autumn of 1066,
           during an attack of Coptic Gadfly on the
           Knack-eeeeee.

KAK   Yes, yes, needn't go back that far. How
           do you spell Knack-ee?

FORTNUM   I don't. Could you – er –

KAK   Oh, I'm sorry. (*He re-agitates the feather*)
           Now tell me something more recent.

FORTNUM   Well if you must know, everything was
           going swimmingly until they dropped this
           terrible . . .

           **Sound of mule raspberries. Groans.
           Everybody on stage leaps up and starts
           swiping at invisible flying things. The
           PIANIST, who up to now has been
           reading a paper behind drawn curtains,
           pulls back the curtains and launches into
           a furious version of 'When the Lights go
           on again'. At the same time a SMALL**

MAN in a leopard skin, Army boots, great ginger wig (and it must be ENORMOUS) and great red beard, enters with a great club with which he batters the stage in a frenzy. The noise stops, the LITTLE MAN exits in tears. PIANIST pulls the curtains on his platform. All reverts to normal.

KAK   The H-bomb?

FORTNUM   Yes, that's the one. Ever since then, I've been strangely troubled.

KAK   Did the noise keep you awake?

FORTNUM   No, I slept like a log, I do tree impressions as well. When I came to I discovered a marked change. As was my wont I toddled along for lunch at the Constitutional Club, and it had gone – rubble, nothing but rubble, and such small portions. I saw Lord Hailsham standing outside stark naked waving a Union Jack and shouting 'Vive le Sport'. I could see his membership had lapsed, so I ignored him. I wrote a stiff letter to The Times, then, they broke the news to me. While I'd been asleep, they'd had World War III. (*Walks forward, looks up*) I didn't get a chance to join the regiment.

KAK   There, there – that part of it came as quite a shock to me too; fortunately I managed to get there in time for a disability pension.

FORTNUM Well, since the bomb I haven't eaten a thing.

KAK Why not?

FORTNUM (*annoyed*) Can't afford it! Bread at sixty-four gns per fine ounce. See this? (*Shows signet ring*) I had this bit of bread mounted this morning.

KAK Gad, beautifully cut.

FORTNUM removes ring and holds it out to KAK.

FORTNUM Look, Doctor, all this, if you'll give me a prescription to alleviate malnutrition.

KAK Right! (*Writes on pad*) T grams Brown Windsor Soup. Eggs and Chips. Jam and Custard. There, I want you to take this three time a day before meals, any good restaurant will make it up.

FORTNUM I'll try Boots Café.

KAK Good, anything else?

FORTNUM Yes, ever since they dropped this bomb, I've had the morbid fear I might turn into a Bedsitting Room.

Here the actors must introduce great tension.

KAK   A Bedsitting Room?

FORTNUM   Yes!

KAK   Will you be empty? I – er – I mean – how would you visualise yourself as the Bedsitting Room?

FORTNUM   A brick wall with brick wallpaper over it. A plastic draining board, fluorescent lighting, red bakelite door knobs and an outside wooden karzi. Oh dear, what should I do?

KAK   Well, I think you ought to stick out for thirty shillings a week — at a push you might get two quid.

FORTNUM   Two quids??? Look, you're not getting the point, I don't want to be *a* Bed *Sitting Room*. You can't have a Lord turning into that sort of thing. Woburn Abbey, Blenheim Palace, where the takings are reasonable, but a bed sit at two quids?

KAK   You sound quite *Ad*-Amant about that.

FORTNUM   I am *Ad*-Amant. I am.

KAK   You sound quite Adamant about that *Ad*-Amant.

FORTNUM   I am. I am. (*Stresses*)

KAK   Look, let's be practical – have you seen a good estate agent?

FORTNUM   Yes. (*Full of meaning*) He was quite quite beautiful.

KAK   (*worried*) What?

FORTNUM   But he refused to handle me until I'd become this blasted Bed Sit. Two quid. The fool didn't realise, I'll do anything to stave off the prospect of becoming a Bed Sit. I'll pay anything . . . even . . . (*He produces a gold coin*) . . . even Money!

Black out, divine spotlight from directly overhead on KAK. Sound of Hallelujah Chorus by Handel (vocal chorus). FORTNUM gives him the coin, KAK bends his head in relief. Lights up. Music stops. KAK to his feet.

KAK   Well, well, Lord Fortnum, I think we can do business. Roll up your sleeve.

FORTNUM rolls up sleeve.

FORTNUM   Gad! An arm.

KAK   Say Ah.

FORTNUM   Ahhhh.

KAK   Good, you can get dressed again.

FORTNUM turns modestly away to pull down sleeve.

KAK   Now, I want you to start taking these Anti Bed Sit Pills; take six a day, one every half mile.

FORTNUM   But I only live a mile away.

KAK   You'll have to move further out, then.

FORTNUM   But I . . .

Heavy hammering on side of theatre. In event of there being no side door near stage, a hand protrudes from the wings and beckons KAK. KAK opens the door or reaches the beckoning hand. Immediately a parking meter is thrust in front of him and 'MATE', the parking meter attendant, enters. Old cloth cap, ragged overcoat, zip-up boot slippers, large iron-frame spectacles, old, about fifty-five, unshaven, long hair. He has a packet of Daz slung around his shoulders.

MATE   You can't park here, sir.

He writes a parking ticket, puts it in coffin.

MATE   This should cost him a fortune. I –

He suddenly is taken by the large packet of Lux which LORD FORTNUM has slung around his shoulder. FORTNUM tries to slide the packet out of sight.

MATE   Hold it, hold, hold, that's this then. Ohhhhhh. Wearing Lux in a Daz area. Eh oh oh ho ho ho.

Writes a ticket.

MATE   I shall have to report you to the Daz Committee, sir. Not to mention Bazonka.

FORTNUM   Bazonka?

MATE   I told you not to mention that, sir. I shall have to charge you . . .

(From the play *The Bedsitting Room*,
first performed at the Mermaid Theatre in 1963)

BARRY HUMPHRIES

Barry Humphries believes that supernatural intervention led to his working with Spike Milligan, after his spectacular comedy career had initially faltered on his arrival in England from Australia. But he also reveals that taking a curtain call with Spike could lead to some embarrassing moments.

It was in Sydney in the early sixties that I first met Spike Milligan. At the time, I was performing my first one man show in a small theatre, when I was told the famous Goon was in the audience. He came backstage later and we soon became friends.

A couple of years later, I was appearing at Peter Cook's Establishment Club, in Soho, without too much success. My engagement was cut short and since my wife was expecting our first child, I suffered some considerable economic anxiety. At a friend's suggestion, I even consulted a well-known psychic lady in Belsize Park, who told me that I had no worries about the future, because I would be receiving a telegram with good news.

Sure enough, the next day a telegram arrived ... from Spike Milligan, offering me the second lead in the play he had written with John Antrobus, 'The Bedsitting Room'. The show had opened successfully at the Mermaid, but was transferring to the Comedy and Graham Stark had dropped out of the cast.

Spike on stage in this show gave the funniest performance I had ever seen or have seen since. But he had a habit, at curtain call, of not merely introducing the cast to the audience, but enumerating their intimate domestic problems and moral vulnerabilities.

Thus, one actor who was in the habit of issuing dud cheques was embarrassingly singled out and the audience adjured never to lend him money. Another well-known former Shakespearean was obliged to stand uncomfortably on stage in long underwear, while Spike regaled the audience with private details of his marital problems.

Spike was always conscious of the absurdities and pretensions of theatrical life and he took an anarchic Irishman's delight in pillorying 'English dignity', and the pretensions of the shabby genteel.

It is a special privilege to able to celebrate the life and gifts of a man who is still with us and still contributing to the well-being of the human race. I regard myself as a fortunate man to know him.

POETRY

HAVE A NICE DAY!

'Help, help,' said a man, 'I'm drowning.'
'Hang on,' said a man from the shore.
'Help, help,' said the man, 'I'm not clowning.'
'Yes, I know, and I heard you before.
Be patient, dear man who is drowning.
You see, I've got a disease.
I'm waiting for a Doctor J. Browning,
So do be patient, please.'
'How long,' said the man who was drowning,
'Will it take for the Doc to arrive?'
'Not very long,' said the man with the disease.
'Till then try staying alive.'
'Very well,' said the man who was drowning,
'I'll try and stay afloat
By reciting poems of Browning
And other things he wrote.'

'Help, help,' said the man who had a disease,
'I suddenly feel quite ill.'
'Keep calm,' said the man who was drowning,
'Breathe deeply and lay quite still.'
'Oh dear,' said the man with the awful disease,
'I think I'm going to die.'
'Farewell,' said the man who was drowning.
Said the man with the disease, 'Goodbye.'
So the man who was drowning drowned
And the man with the disease passed away,
But apart from that and a fire in my flat
It's been a very nice day.

MONKEY

Monkey, monkey, monkey,
Sitting in a tree,
Pulling funny faces –
Please pull one for me.
Pull one for my daddy,
Pull one for my mum,
But when it comes to teacher
Turn round and show yer bum!

(From the book *Startling Verse for all the Family*, 1987)

THE WHITE FLAG

The two great Generals and the two great Armies faced each other across one great battlefield. The two great Generals marched about their two great Armies as they faced each other across one great battlefield. The two great Generals marched about their two great Armies as they faced each other across one great battlefield. One great general said to himself, 'We can't hold out against this other great Army much longer,' and the other great general said, 'We can't hold out against this other Army much longer,' so the first great General said to one of his great Sergeants, 'Hoist a white flag'.

Private Fred Lengths was commanded by one great General to haul up a flag. At the same time, Private Norrington Blitt had also been signalled by his General to hoist their white flag, and so the two great Armies stood surrendering to each other across the battlefield. It was very quiet, and the two white flags were the only movement seen.

Three days passed, and one great general said, 'What's happened?', as did the other great General. Both great Generals were informed that each side had surrendered to the other. 'Impossible,' said the first General.

'It can't be true,' said the second General.

'My arms are aching,' said Private Blitt, as did Private Lengths.

'How long have they had their flag up?' said the first great General.

'Three days,' at which time the second great General had asked the same question, and received the same answer.

'Tell them *we* surrendered – *first*!'

'The message was shouted across the great battlefield.

'No, no,' was the reply, 'We surrendered first.' Neither side wanted to lose the initiative. Stalemate.

The two great Generals met in a tent in the middle of the field. 'According to my notes,' said the first, 'our flag went up at one minute to eleven on the 1st April.'

'So did ours,' was the reply.

'But,' said the first General, 'I gave the order to put the white flag up at a quarter to eleven . . .' and was met with the same reply. Stalemate II.

The first General screwed his eyes up, screwed his knees up, his nose, teeth and ears. 'Tell you what – my peace flag is whiter than yours.'

'Nonsense,' was the furious reply. 'Hold ours up to the light – not a stain in sight. We use the Bluinite.'

'Bluinite!' guffawed the facing General. 'My dear fellow, Rinso, the new white Rinso, is my answer to you. That's why I say my flag is whiter.'

'The window test!' they said simultaneously.

In due course, a window was brought, against which the two flags were held. Alas, both were of the same degree and intensity. Stalemate III.

Meantime the makers of Bluinite and Rinso had heard of the conflict.

'You aren't going to let that lot get away with it,' said the managing director of Bluinite to the first General, at which time, as you can guess, Sir Jim Rinso was inciting the second General.

'I will prove who surrendered first,' he said, as the first great atomic blast exterminated them.

(From the book *A Dustbin Of Milligan*, 1961)

POETRY FROM NORMA FARNES

JOURNEY

I think I am going out of my mind
The journey shouldn't take long
Once I get outside I'll be fine
I won't have to worry about thinking
I'll sit on a green bank of Sodium Amytal
   and watch my mind float away
Ah! My mind was a visitor!
A white-washed nurse
   a tray of NHS food
If only it would fit my mind
It's my stomach they're treating
   letting my head starve to death.

(January 1981. From the book *The Mirror Running*, 1987)

MANIC DEPRESSION

The pain is too much
A thousand grim winters
  grow in my head
In my ears
  the sound of the
  coming dead.
All seasons
All sane
All living
All pain.
No opiate to lock still
  my senses
Only left,
  the body locked tenses.

(St Luke's Hospital Psychiatric Wing, 1953/4)

THE NEW ROSE

The new rose
  trembles with early beauty
The babe sees the beckoning carmine
  the tiny hand
  clutches the cruel stem.
The babe screams
The rose is silent –
Life is already telling lies.

(Orme Court, London, February 1967)

CHRISTMAS 1970

A little girl called Silé Javotte
Said 'look at the lovely presents I've got'
While a little girl in Biafra said
'Oh, what a lovely slice of bread'.

FRETWORK, THE SHAME OF OUR CITIES

Hercules 'Fred' Bleriote snuggled down in his favourite chair. He was a tall man, as you, dear reader will notice when he stands up. Hercules puffed casually on his cherry-wood samovar, a wisp of smoke escaped from the bowl, he imediately inserted a fresh wisp. Lazily he drew on his pipe, he drew on the wall, the ceiling the soles of his boots, was there no end to this man's ability?

The time was six-thirty and France was at war. To all outward appearances he was at peace, but a quick X-Ray shows his inward appearance differed drastically. (Just hold this page up to the light, you'll see what I mean.) Hercules was in a state of acute agitation, on the table before him lay a freshly opened letter which he was even *now* freshly reading . . . 'Your mistress Madame Legerts (if you pronounce that right it should sound like "My dam leg hurts": this is a desperate attempt to make you laugh) is in our hands, do not tell the police or she will meet a fate worse than death. Wrap ten million francs around a brown paper parcel, stand on top of the Sacre Coeur, and sing the third act of Rigoletto.'

Hercules clutched the back of his forehead, he reeled sideways, and finally reeled upright. A sudden second sense told him danger was nigh. With one tigerish bound he leapt behind the fire screen, not a moment too soon. A mere eight hours later a brick landed on the very spot he had vacated. I should like to mention that a brick also hit him the moment he leapt behind the fire screen. He grabbed the phone: 'Le Police' he gabbled in fluent French. In a matter of seconds the Maria Noire was knocking at the door; out sprang a tall handsome cross-eyed Gendarme followed by trente-deux (34) French policemen, who immediately gesticulated in a corner. They advanced on Hercules, led in the middle by a short bearded detective, wearing the uniform of a plain clothes detective. He doffed his hat, teeth, gloves, boots and fired a pistol in the air. 'We are Le Police,' he said with an air of authority. 'Thank heaven you've arrived,' cried Hercules. As one man the police looked heavenwards and exclaimed, 'Thank you, heaven.' It was 6.32 and France was at war. Hercules pointed towards a direction, 'Come in, make yourselves at home.' They accepted the invitation and in a trice, several were in the garden drinking wine, two were upstairs sleeping softly with the blinds drawn, the rest sat around the house hitting each other and making little raffia mats. It was now seven o'clock and France was at war!

A RACE TO THE DEATH AND BACK AGAIN WITH ONLY ONE TEA BREAK!

Next morning the bearded dectective appeared on the landing wearing Hercules' best dressing gown. 'Quelle belle jour,' he announced. After breakfast of frogs and porridge, he cornered Hercules. 'Why are you keeping us all a prisoner in your own house?' Hercules blanched blanche, he advanced on the bearded Detective and thrust the ransom note under his nose. 'Why did you thrust that note under my nose?' asked the detective. 'It's not under my nose, it's under yours, it's the way this story's written that makes it confusing.' (How dare he! That's the last time he's in a story of mine – signed Spike Milligan) ... The bearded detective read the ransom note. '*Sacre bleu*, this note is no concern of ours, it's addressed to you.'

'But M'sieur Detective, I phoned you because I was in trouble.'

'What a nerve, when we're in trouble, do we phone you? Huh, no M'sieur, this is a job for the police.' And by God dear reader so it was, join the police and help. It was now four-forty and France was at war!

Author's note: I know this story lacks that vital something, but what the hell.

(From the book *A Dustbin Of Milligan*, 1961)

THE CASE OF THE MUKKINESE BATTLEHORN

IN THE WONDER OF SCHIZOPHRENOSCOPE – THE NEW SPLIT SCREEN

(Screen tears in two to reveal . . .)

Scene	Night. Swirling fog. Nothing is visible through the fog except more fog.
F.X.	Heavy, lung-congested, phlem-ridden, smog-city type coughing
NASAL YANK VOICE OVER	London . . .
F.X.	More gob-hurtling, stomach-churning, snot-bucket, etc coughing
N.Y.V.O.	Yes, London. Who can fail to recognise the city's great landmarks? In Trafalgar Square, for instance, there is Nelson's

Column and even in the fog you cannot
miss Nelson's Column . . .

F.X.   **Screech of tyres, horrendous
scrunching smashing everything to
smithereens noise**

N.Y.V.O.   You see? There's someone not missing
it now, but there is one famous
landmark which anyone could miss . . .

Scene   **Exterior shots of Scotland yard**

N.Y.V.O.   . . . recognise it? Scotland Yard.
Scotland Yard is the headquarters of
the CID – the Criminal Investigations
Department of the London Police.

Scene   **Battered filing cabinet is opened by pair
of battered hands which retrieve
battered file.**

N.Y.V.O.   Let us look at the world famous CID at
work through the medium of a true
real-life case . . .
(*Hands place file on table displaying
the label 'The Case Of The Mukkinese
Battlehorn'*)

N.Y.V.O.   . . . a factual documentary record
straight from the files of Scotland Yard
. . .

Scene   **Night. Close-up of display cabinet in
museum bearing the plaque
'Metropolitan Museum. Mukkinese**

Battlehorn. 9th Century. Copper Inlaid With Rubies And Emeralds.'

N.Y.V.O.   ... yes, The Case of The Mukkinese Battlehorn.
(*Crescendo of dramatic music. Pan back from the cabinet as a house brick is lobbed into the shot, smashing the glass. Running footsteps. Black gloved hands retrieve the brick, dusting it down. Running footsteps as 'black gloves' makes off ... pause ... running footsteps as 'black gloves' returns, drops brick and makes off with the Battlehorn!*)

Scene   **Day. Elderly janitor in uniform enters museum strolling towards broken display case. Pauses when he sees the case, clutches heart and staggers towards phone.**

N.Y.V.O.   The theft was not discovered until the following morning ...
(*Dramatic music. Janitor winds handle on side of phone then gasps into mouthpiece.*)

JANITOR   Get me Scotland Yard!

Scene   **Day. Police car races through streets.**

N.Y.V.O.   Within minutes of the report of the burglary, the CID was on the scene in the person of Scotland yard's ace detective Superintendent Quilt.

Scene   Day. Museum exterior. Police car
          shoots past and out of shot.

F.X.   Screech of tyres. Car reversing noise.

Scene   Car shoots backwards past museum
          entrance. Quilt disembarks from the
          rear door, remonstrates with the driver,
          pointing forward towards the entrance.
          Car moves forward, Quilt walks
          alongside chastising driver. Car stops
          and Quilt opens boot to let out
          Sergeant Brown.

Scene   Day. Museum interior. Enter Quilt and
          Brown who walk past an attractive
          female police constable standing guard
          near the door.

POLICE-   Good morning, sir.
WOMAN

QUILT   Good morning, Constable. Where's the
          body?

POLICE-   Body, sir? There's no body here.
WOMAN

QUILT   (*Amorously*) You mean . . . we're
          alone?

N.Y.V.O. Wasting no time, Superintendent Quilt
          and Sergeant Brown began a thorough
          search for clues.

Scene	Museum interior. Entrance to display case area. Quilt and Brown enter. Quilt pulls a magnifying glass from his pocket and studies an ornament intently. Behind him, Brown bends over, pointing dramatically to the floor with one hand and dramatically to the ceiling with the other.
BROWN	look, sir! An impression of a heel!
QUILT	Very clever, Brown, but we haven't time for your impressions now. *(They walk further into the room and confront a tweed-jacketed character studying a bust with an eye glass.)*
QUILT	I say, there. Are you the body?
MAN	No, are you?
QUILT	Oh, no. I'm Superintendent Quilt of Scotland Yard.
MAN	Delighted to meet you. My name's Nodule. I'm the curator here. *(They shake hands cordially, saying 'How do you do'. Nodule returns to studying the bust. Something off camera catches Quilt's eye.)*
QUILT	Hello . . .
NODULE	Hello? I thought we'd just met? *(Quilt brushes him aside and heads for the Battlehorn display case.)*

QUILT   What's all this about, eh?

NODULE   That? Oh, we had a robbery last night.

QUILT   A robbery? Was anything stolen?
         (*He picks up the display case card.*)

QUILT   Well, well. 'Metropolitan Museum.
         Mukkinese Battlehorn. 9th Century.
         Copper Inlaid With Rubies And
         Emeralds'? Ha! You've been swindled,
         old man . . .

NODULE   What?

QUILT   (*Picks brick out of display case.*) Yes!
         This is an ordinary house brick!

NODULE   (*Examines brick with eyeglass.*) I
         know! The Mukkinese Battlehorn has
         been stolen!

QUILT   What?
         (*He drops brick with sickening thud on
         Nodule's foot.*)

NODULE   Aaaaaaaaaaaaaaargh!

QUILT   I must warn you that everything you
         say will be taken down and used in
         evidence against you. Sergeant Brown!

BROWN   Yes, sir!

QUILT   Make a note of all that.

BROWN   Yes, sir . . .
         (*They all babble incoherently together*

for several seconds making no sense whatsoever.)

NODULE . . . straight away!

QUILT Got all that?

BROWN No.

QUILT Good. It strikes me as very fishy why the thief chose this Mukkinese Battlehorn thingy when there were all these other rare and valuable items lying around.

NODULE Really?

QUILT Mmmmmm . . . such as those golden slave bangles . . .

NODULE By jove you're right! He could have whipped one of those Chinese Jade ornaments . . . or even this!
(*Points off camera and walks out of shot, looking back as he talks. Camera pans back to wider shot and we see that he is pointing at and walking towards a vase set on a tall pedestal.*)

NODULE This priceless Grecian vase.
(*Knocks vase off pedestal. It smashes to eensy weensy little bits on the floor.*)

NODULE Botheration! Cleggit!
(*Enter museum guard in uniform.*)

CLEGGIT Yes, sir?

NODULE Pop down to Woolworths and get me another of those priceless Grecian vases.
(*Cleggit salutes and exits.*)

QUILT Nodule, can you give me a full description of this Mukkinese Battlehorn?

NODULE I can do better than that. Cleggit!

VOICE OFF Yes, sir?

NODULE Bring in the other Mukkinese Battlehorn!

QUILT The other?

NODULE Yes. This one was one of a pair. Supposed to be the only identical pair in existence.

QUILT Come now, Mr Nodule. Do you take me for a raving idiot?

NODULE Well, now you mention it, I . . .

QUILT (*Outraged.*) I beg your pardon? I am an officer of the police force and . . .
(*Quilt and Brown gasp with terror as Cleggit enters pointing the fearsome Mukkinese Battlehorn directly at them.*)

QUILT So . . . this is it is it?

NODULE   (*Entranced by the Battlehorn.*) Yes, this . . . is . . . it . . .

BROWN   It sort of looks like a trumpet, sir.

NODULE   Yes, but with a little more plumbing, of course.

QUILT   Tell me, what are these holes?

NODULE   (*Demonstrating*) I'm glad you noticed that. They're for changing the pitch of the note. This is for C sharp . . .

QUILT   That's rather ingenious . . .

NODULE   And that one there is for A flat.

BROWN   Devilishly cunning. What's this slot here for?

NODULE   Used razor blades.

QUILT   Mr Nodule! You're trying to be funny, sir!

NODULE   Aren't we all?

Scene   **Police car racing through the streets.**

N.Y.V.O.   Soon the various experts of the CID began appearing on the scene. At 11.10 the police photographers arrived . . .

Scene   **Car draws up outside museum.**

N.Y.V.O.   . . . photographed the police . . .

Scene   **Charming group shot of the officers inside the museum posing for a picture.**

N.Y.V.O.   ... and hurried away again. At 11.30 Inspector Quilt began his interrogation of witnesses and possible suspects.

Scene   **Quilt and Brown sit at a desk in the museum. Uniformed Constable stands by them. Brown examines the desk quite thoroughly with his magnifying glass.**

QUILT   Send in the night watchman, J. Smith.

CONSTABLE   Yes, sir! Call J. Smith!

Scene   **Sarcophagus opens on the other side of the room and the gormless night watchman steps out, dressed like a village idiot.**

SMITH   Haaaaaaaaaaallo ... (*looking around the room*) Fine, fine, fine, fine ... aaaaah duggo bubby felba noggy (talks complete rubbish).
(*Constable grabs Smith by the arm and escorts him, protesting inconherently, to the desk. Smith gives the Constable a defiant up and down look. Quilt examines Smith through a magnifying glass. Smith pushes his face right up to the other side of the glass to study Quilt.*)

QUILT   Are you J. Smith?

SMITH   Nope, nope, nope.

QUILT   (*to Brown*) He's not J. Smith, Brown!

SMITH   (*to Constable*) He'd nud J. Smith-Brown!

QUILT   (*to Smith*) That's not Brown!

SMITH   (*to Constable*) Dat's nud Brown!

QUILT   Where were you on the night of the troventeenth?

SMITH   I was at da pictures. (*In Constable's ear as though he's deaf*) I was at do pictures!!!! (*In Quilt's face*) Bang! Da cowboy went Bang!! Bang!!! Bang!!!! Bang!!!!! Der-dee-dum-de-dee-dum-de-deyeeee!

QUILT   What about the Mukkinese Battlehorn?

SMITH   (*Nose to nose with Quilt*) Whuddu bout do Mukkinese Baddlehorn?

QUILT   It's been stolen.

SMITH   Ooooooooooooooooooooh. (*In Constable's ear*) Id been shtolen . . .

QUILT   Constable! Get this idiot out of here!

SMITH   Ged do idiot outta here! Ged ridda me! Ged ridda me!
(*Smith exits, dragged off by the*

Constable. Enter Crimp, the ancient janitor who called in Scotland Yard.)

BROWN   Next witness is Mr Crimp the janitor, sir.

QUILT   Mr Crimp, would you like to tell us your story?

CRIMP   Yes, sir. Well, I was proceeding in an orderly manner towards the main gate last night in order to lock up when suddenly somebody jumps up and wallops me on the 'ead. Wallop! Wallop!! Wallop!!! on me 'ead. I turns round and Wallop! Wallop!! Wallop!!! again. Down I goes and Wallop! Wallop!! Wallop!!! on me 'ead again! Then, just as I tried to get up – Wallop! Wallop!! Wallop!!!

QUILT   On your head?

CRIMP   Yes, sir . . . wallop.

QUILT   Wallop?

CRIMP   Wallop.

QUILT   (*Disbelievingly*) Hmmmm . . . tell me Mr Crimp, did you notice anything unusual about these men?

CRIMP   Yes, sir.

QUILT   What?

CRIMP   They kept wallopin' me on me 'ead.

QUILT   Is there anyting else?

CRIMP   Yes, sir. (*Removes hat to reveal massive bandage wrapped round his head.*) Could I have an aspirin?

QUILT   Constable, look after Mr Crimp. (*Crimp exits assisted by constable and next witness is called. Beautiful blonde in sexy dress enters unseen by Quilt and Brown. Brown is finishing his notes watched by Quilt.*)

BROWN   Wallop?

QUILT   Yes. I think that was it. (*Brown looks up and squeals with amazement at the sight of the blonde.*)

BROWN   The next witness is waiting, sir.

QUILT   Right, Brown. Now then sir . . . (*He looks up to see the blonde standing in front of the desk and completely loses his marbles, obviously suffering from instant unrest in the trouser department.*)

QUILT   Er . . . ahem! Harumph!! Ah . . . where were you on the night of the troventeenth?

WOMAN   (*In a mysterious sensuous, suggestive sort of way*) Don't you remember?

QUILT (*Now hot under the collar as well as below the belt*) Have you got all that down, Brown?

BROWN Yes, sir!

QUILT Rub it all out again would you?

Scene **Police car racing through streets.**

N.Y.V.O. Superintendent Quilt hurried back to Scotland Yard and within minutes the well-oiled machinery of the CID sprang into action . . .

Scene **Two convicts in a room. One pedals like mad on a bicycle to generate power for a ramshackle radio which is being operated by his ramshackle mate.**

RADIO CON Calling patrol car 11d. Urgent! Turn left into Oxford Street and head west!

Scene **Car 11d responds as instructed.**

RADIO CON Calling patrol car 5k. Turn right into Oxford Street and head due east!

F.X. **Screech of tyres and thunderous crunch of cars crashing into each other.**

RADIO CON (*Winces*) Calling ambulance one seven! Calling ambulance one seven . . .

N.Y.V.O. The search continued. During the afternoon several arrests were made.

Scene **Stock newsreel footage of thousands of**

German POWs being marched across the desert escorted by an armoured car.

N.Y.V.O.   With nightfall the weather took a turn for the worse, but even in the darkest, foggiest street London's indomitable police searched on, stopping wayfarers and ruthlessly questioning them . . .

Scene   **Police Constable approaches courting couple on foggy street corner. They are standing under a streetlight, otherwise they would not be visible.**

CONSTABLE   Hey! You two!

MAN   Yes?

CONSTABLE   Can you tell me the way back to the police station?

MAN   (*Points*) It's just over there.

CONSTABLE   Thank you. (*Exits with arms outstretched to feel his way.*)

F.X.   **Horrendous scream and loud splash of a body hitting the water.**

GIRL   Darling, how romantic. We must be near the river . . .

N.Y.V.O.   By noon the following day, vast amounts of vital evidence were pouring in.

Scene   Constable enters Quilt's office at Scotland Yard carrying a huge mound of envelopes and papers. He approaches Quilt and Brown who look up expectantly. Constable plucks one tiny envelope off the top of the pile, tosses it on Quilt's desk and leaves. Brown snatches the envelope and examines it with his magnifying glass.

BROWN   (*Triumphantly*) Aha! It's a letter, sir!

QUILT   Good work, Brown. (*Opens letter*) Hello . . . it's a report from the police laboratory. 'Analysis of fluff taken from night watchman's trouser cuff. Discovered were fragments of wool, cotton, fine ash from a Turkish-type cigarette, particles of mud from a limestone district . . .

BROWN   Good heavens!

QUILT   . . . and a quantity of low grade industrial soot and coal dust.'

BROWN   Really, sir? And what were the analysis's conclusions?

QUILT   'This suit needs cleaning.' (*Holds out letter in left hand*) File that, would you, Brown?

BROWN   At once, sir! (*Reaches into drawer, pulls out a nail file and manicures*

Quilt's left hand.)
(There is a knock at the door and a
gentleman enters to the
accompaniment of corny silent movie
piano music. He is wearing Victorian
garb and gesticulates wildly, apparently
unable to speak.)

CAPTION   'Good morning.'
(He waves, indulges in fantasy
swordplay, acknowledges non-existent
applause and bows.)

CAPTION   'I am Catchpole Burkington, famous
star of silent films.'
(Quilt tries to speak but nothing comes
out. Only corny piano music can be
heard. He writes on a piece of paper.)

CAPTION   What do you want?
(Catchpole mimes grief, humility,
disgrace.)

CAPTION   'I've come for my unemployment
money.'
(Quilt and Brown look at each other
and write out another note.)

CAPTION   The Labour Exchange is next door!!
(Catchpole mimes gratitude, exits into
a cupboard marked 'Disguises', does a
quick change to reappear in a bathing
costume, exits again to change back
then finishes with a huge bow in front

of the office door whereupon the
Constable enters with another mound
of papers and falls over him.)

N.Y.V.O. Six months later the public are pressing
for an early arrest. Assistant
Commissioner Sir Jervis Fruit rings
Superintendent Quilt with an urgent
enquiry.

Scene Camp lounge lizard in smoking jacket
relaxing on chaise longue holds
cigarette holder in one hand and
telephone receiver in other.

FRUIT Hello, Quilt? Have you a light?

QUILT (*On phone in his own office.*) A light?
Certainly sir.
(*Quilt produces a lighter, lights it and*
holds it to his telephone mouthpiece.
Fruit holds the cigarette to his
telephone earpiece and lights up.)

FRUIT Thank you. Quilt, about this Mucky
Knees Battle Horn thingy . . .
something must be done, you know. I
want you to call at every music shop
and pawn shop masquerading as a
musician enquiring for a Mucky Knees
Battle Horn. Got that? Good.
Whatever you do, take every
precaution and don't get yourself killed
. . . mmmmm . . . I don't know, though.

Scene   **Quilt's office. There is a crash of breaking glass and an enormous chunk of concrete thuds onto Quilt's desk, arriving there via the window. Quilt falls backwards off his chair.**

QUILT   Brown! What was that?
(*Brown rushes over to examine the concrete with his magnifying glass.*)
Well, what is it?

BROWN   It's a magnifying glass, sir!

QUILT   Control, Brown, control.

BROWN   (*Points to concrete*) Stone! There's a message tied to it, sir!

QUILT   What does it say?

BROWN   'Fred Smith – Window Repairer.'

QUILT   (*Reads note*) '14a Hurley Street'.

BROWN   Why that's 14a Hurley Street's address, sir!

QUILT   Yes, and no more than a stone's throw from here! Brown, we'll start our search there.

Scene   **Three ball pawn shop signs flash on screen. Brown and Quilt are located beneath a <u>four</u> ball sign.**

QUILT   Hmmmm . . . business must be good (*knocks on shop door*). Come on! (*knocks again*)

Scene	**Inside the junk-ridden pawn shop. Continuous knocking noise from the front door. Henry Crun, the proprietor, is offering a saucer of milk to the bell end of a tuba.**
HENRY	Fifi! Fifi! Come out now you naughty little pussle-wussle . . .
MIN'S VOICE OFF	Henry! Henreeeeeee . . .!!
HENRY	Come on, Tiddles. What? What is it, Min? I'm trying . . .
MIN'S VOICE OFF	There's someone at the door knock-knock-knockity-knocking on the door, Henry!
HENRY	Min, I can't hear what you're saying for all that knocking noise. (*They mutter to each other and Henry finally crosses to the door, opening it slightly.*)
HENRY	Would you mind not knocking for a moment, pease?
QUILT	Certainly. (*Henry goes back inside.*)
HENRY	Now what was it, Min?
MIN'S VOICE OFF	There's someone at the door, Henry.
HENRY	No there isn't, Minnie.

MIN'S VOICE
OFF

Oh . . . no, there isn't is there, Henry? Sorry, buddy. Goodnight.

HENRY

Goodnight, Minnie.
(*Crosses back to door and opens it again.*)

HENRY

It's all right. You can carry on, now.

QUILT

Thank you.

HENRY

Thank YOU.
(*He returns to his milk and tuba amidst a thunderous knocking.*)

MIN'S VOICE
OFF

Henreeeeeeeeeeee!!! There's a nicky, knocky noo on the door!

HENRY

There is not a nicky, knocky, nirdle, nardle noo! I'm telling you . . . (*They argue feebly until Henry finally answers the door.*)
Good evening. Won't you please come in? (*Closes door with Quilt and Brown still outside.*)

QUILT

Brown, this may be dangerous. Stick around here and keep your eyes open. (*He enters the shop.*)

Scene

Inside the pawn shop. Quilt approaches Henry who is seated at a work bench.

QUILT

Good evening. I'm thinking of taking up music and I'm looking for a Mukkinese Battlehorn.

HENRY   You can't get them, you know.

QUILT   Why is that?

HENRY   You can't get the wood, you know.

QUILT   I see.

HENRY   Poor old Molly Gnasher.

QUILT   What was the matter with her?

HENRY   She couldn't get the wood either.

QUILT   Ahem ... perhaps some other time.
Good Night.
(*He exits and joins Brown in the street.
They spot the beautiful girl from the
museum leaving the shop.*)

GIRL   Good night, Mother!

MIN'S VOICE OFF   Good night, darling. See you later.

BROWN   Good heavens, sir! Isn't that the lady
we questioned at the museum? I think
we ought to ...
(*With a sigh of infatuation and a dopey
look on his face, Quilt has, in fact,
already set off to follow the girl.*)

N.Y.V.O.   The mysterious blonde led Quilt and
Brown to Maxie's club, a notorious
hang-out for London's underworld ...

Scene   **Quilt and Brown approach a heavy,
studded door inset with a barred,**

head-sized window at eye level. They pause, Quilt begins to issue instructions to Brown and the window opens sharply to reveal the face of a heavily bearded man.

BEARDED MAN   Yeah?

QUILT   I haven't knocked yet.

BEARDED MAN   Sorry.
(*He closes the window. Quilt knocks. Window opens.*)

BEARDED MAN   Yeah?

QUILT   Are you Mr Maxie?

BEARDED MAN   Such is my name.

QUILT   Sorry to bother you, Mr Such. Will Mr Maxie be long?

BEARDED MAN   I am Mr Maxie.

QUILT   Then you weren't very long then, were you? We were wondering if we could get into your club here.

BEARDED MAN   No.

QUILT   Why not?

BEARDED MAN	This is the specially fitted, reinforced, double-strength, armour-plated door and <u>nobody</u> can get in here.
QUILT	Then how did you get in?
BEARDED MAN	Easy, I came through here. (*He points out of shot and the camera pans round to reveal saloon style louvred swing doors.*)
QUILT	Cunning, very cunning. (*A body hurtles out through the doors.*)
QUILT	Anyone we know?
BROWN	No. sir.
QUILT	Brown, you better stick around and see what clues you can find. (*Quilt enters the smokey club. Various villainous types sit at saloon-style tables and a band in the corner plays vigorous trad. jazz. Music and conversation stops as he walks in. He crosses the room to sit at a table next to the blonde and the music restarts, changing to middle eastern pipe music. To Quilt's delight, a many-veiled dancer appears. He smiles lustfully as the dancer sways alluringly towards him. The dancer smooches up to him closer than a veil's breadth.*)

QUILT   Oh, bounteous one. Oh, fairest of the
        fair. Oh, sublime siren. Oh, exquisite
        enchantress. What are you doing in a
        low hovel like this?
        (*The dancer raises the face veil.*)

SMITH   I godda make a livin', too, ya know!

QUILT   You! But you're not a girl, you're a
        man!

SMITH   I know dat! But don't tell da manager.

QUILT   Why not?

SMITH   We're engaged!

QUILT   Ha! I see it all now!

SMITH   You can't. I ain't taken da veils off yet!
        (*Smith exits mumbling a lunatic chant
        and Brown enters.*)

BROWN   I say, sir. Wasn't that dancer the man
        we interviewed at the museum?

QUILT   Yes. And that's not all, Brown. At last I
        begin to see the whole sinister plot.

BROWN   What do you mean, sir?

QUILT   I'll show you. Waiter! Bring me the
        manager.

BEARDED   Somebody call me?
MAN

QUILT   Ah, yes! First the nightwatchman and then . . . (*rips off disguise beard*)

BROWN   Good heavens, sir! The curator of the museum!

QUILT   Yes! Alias Doppleganger Wormscrew, head of an international ring of Mukkinese Battlehorn smugglers!

WORMSCREW   Curses! Unmasked! Waiter!

BROWN   Careful, sir! This might be a devilish trick!
(*Waiter delivers a soup tureen. Wormscrew whips off the lid and plucks a revolver from the soup.*)

QUILT   Gads! Minestrone!

BROWN   (*Touches gun and tastes finger.*) And no salt!

QUILT   Quick, Brown!
(*Brown opens his raincoat to reveal two swords.*)

QUILT   The eleventh hour but nevertheless in the nick of time!
(*Quilt chooses a sword.*)

WORMSCREW   Bah! Outwitted by an Eton audacious trick!

QUILT   Enough! Come – touché!

WORMSCREW   Three-ché!

(*They fence, Wormscrew using the revolver like a sword. Brown, holding Quilt's hat, looks inside it.*)

BROWN   Good heavens! He's gone!

QUILT   Touché!

WORMSCREW   Three-ché!

QUILT   Four-ché!
(*In the midst of a clinch, Quilt snatches a bottle of ketchup from the table. He daubs some on Wormscrew's sleeve. They break and Wormscrew notices his red stained sleeve.*)

WORMSCREW   Oh, blood! (*faints*)

QUILT   There! That's put an end to your nefarious activities. Nothing can save you now. Not even all the king's horses and all the king's men.
(*Fanfare sounds. Clattering of hooves. The Three Musketeers burst in and salute with their swords.*)

MUSKETEERS   Fred for king!

QUILT   Brown, help me!

BROWN   (*Leaps forward, drawing his sword.*)
Excalibur, sir!
(*Massive swordfight ensues involving everyone in the club. Doppleganger lies on the floor moaning 'I'm dying!' Quilt*)

finds himself fencing with the beautiful blonde.)

QUILT   Brown! Who is this girl?

BROWN   That's the producer's girlfriend, sir! (*to camera*) You think I'm kidding? (*The swordfight rages on with cries of 'Have at you!'; 'No, have at you!', 'I'm dying!' and 'I know, it's in the script!' Finally, Quilt and Brown are slung out into the street through the swing doors. Bruised and bloodied, they land in a heap in the gutter, although there is no sign of whoever made the heap.*)

QUILT   I fear that taught them a lesson, Brown.

BROWN   By jove, yes, sir!

QUILT   Thank goodness I've got you, Brown. It would take a superman to evade those eagle eyes of yours. Come, lad, we must find the Mukkinese Battlehorn. (*They walk off along the street passing a busker who is playing the Mukkinese Batlehorn and wearing an 'Ex-Mukkinese Serviceman' notice around his neck. Quilt and Brown look him up and down but fail to recognise the massive Battlehorn.*)

QUILT   Give him a copper coin, Brown. (*They exit*)

CLOSING CAPTIONS:	By Special Arrangement with Nathan Twitt esq.

Those who did not appear are ...

Freda Clench the under-water soprano (Own Tank)

Fred Nurke

Jim Pills Saxophonist Extraordinary

Barbara Seville

and

Lurgi the Wonder Dog

(From the 1956 film starring Spike Milligan, Peter Sellers and Dick Emery)

THE SHEEPDOG TRIAL

It was one of those days, that's how they come in
Ireland, in ones, in ones, in those, in days, yes, it was
one of those one days when you could smell fried eggs,
it was that kind of day for Charlie McCafferty, he was
up before the lark. Normally he was up before the
Magistrate, the usual, drunk, drunk in charge, drunk
in charge of a donkey, sober in charge of a drunk
donkey, and, he could smell fried eggs, the Magistrate
had cautioned him, 'You must give it up,' he said.
'Jasus, I have,' said McCafferty, 'you should ha' seen
me when I was really on it', and fried eggs.

Yes, it was one of those days. He arose at five-thirty
in time to turn the alarm off before it woke him up, he
leapt from his bed, opened the window, took a deep
breath, ah! he could smell fried eggs. Raising his skinny
arms heavenwards, revealing hairy armpits like rela-
tives of the nudist woman with a fanny like a deserted
crow's nest, plunging down he touched his toes, ah!

fried eggs! Next, like Dr Jekyll, he started to change for the big day. Today was the Drool and District Sheepdog Trials. Now, should he wear this tie? Or that tie? He put on that tie.

In the kitchen his aged one-legged mother Silé hopped around preparing his breakfast, flavoured by ash from her cigarette. Having one leg had its drawbacks, she had to advertise, 'One-legged woman wishes to meet one right-legged woman with a view to buying a pair of shoes.' Silé hopped and hummed a DIY tune, it was to music what Colonel Gadaffi was to medieval brass rubbing.

Like the instructions from a Portolano, the aroma of cooking sailed up the stairs over a sleeping McCafferty, sending the gastric juices whirlygigging in his swonnicles. 'Ah! fried eggs,' he said. Putting a rosary in his waistcoat and a crucifix in his rear trouser pocket (he liked God's protection fore and aft) he sauntered down the stairs. 'By Gor, Mudder, dem fried eggs smell lovely.' He seated himself at the plain wooden table and read the plain wooden *Dublin Times*.

'I see der vote has gone against divorce,' he said. 'Oh, yes,' hopped Silé. It's no good, they'll have to make adultery legal.'

Hopping, his mother transported the sizzling frying pan of bacon and cabbage to the table. He took a mothful then stopped, really he wanted to take a mouthful. 'Dis isn't fried eggs,' he said.

This, dear reader, was his trouble, he could only smell fried eggs, be it ham, turkey, onions, fish, liver, he'd smell fried eggs. The night the hayricks had caught fire he sat up in bed and said, 'I smell fried eggs.' His wife had put on Allure, an expensive perfume. 'Like it?' she said. 'Fried eggs,' said he.

The doctor said there was no cure. 'You've got naso-ovumoderatus syndrome.'

'Oh,' said McCafferty. 'What would that be?'

'That would be five pounds,' said the doctor. 'There's only one cure, have fried eggs every day.'

'I demand a second opinion,' said McCafferty.

The doctor gave it and that was a further five pounds. 'I smell fried eggs,' he said.

The Drool Sheepdog Trials; the day was clear and sunny as they all assembled in Maughan Field. The whole district was out to lay bets, or wimmin. There were three entrants, One, Two and Three; McCafferty, Pat Moloney and Len Byrne.

The two judges were under the oak tree with scorecards, poteen and binoculars, farmers all. If they dropped the atom bomb here now it would wipe out Irish agriculture in the west and the world would be none the wiser. ATOM BOMB DROPPED ON DROOL, NO DAMAGE AT ALL would be the headline.

The Scottish black-faced sheep stood protestant-like midfield in an unsuspecting flock, the first contestant! Charlie McCafferty and his dog Boy, he originally named it Bernard in honour of Shaw, but considering it old-fashioned he named it John after Lennon. Such was his admiration for the Beatles that after a month he called the puzzled dog after McCartney, a month later George, next Ringo, finally Boy after Boy George, a Great honour in Drool. The dog was so paranoid he would answer to any name. Now Bernard-John-Paul-

George-and-Boy sat on his bum in the wet grass looking up at his master wondering what name he was today.

The judges rang a bell, the great Drool Sheepdog Trial was on! At a whistled command, boy set off on a long, looping run to get behind the flock. Apart from the smell of fried eggs, so far so good, the air was filled with the high fluctuating whistles of McCafferty as the dog zig-zagged behind the flock. I'm doin' powerful well, thought McCafferty, but all good things come to an end. Among the starling flocks of Drool was a particularly intelligent one, shall we call him Puck? Puck was a superb mimic; first he mastered the sound of the trimphone that had people running to answer it; for a while now all around the district he had picked up the various shepherds' whistles and was fluent in all of them. It was a moment when McCafferty was on the verge of getting the sheep in the pen that Puck took a hand. Suddenly, inexplicably, Boy drove the sheep in a series of circles, took them off in a northern direction, made them swim a stream, tried to drive them up a tree and despite McCafferty's apoplectic whistles disappeared with them over Maughan Hill.

Drool was stunned. McCafferty sussed it out first. 'It's a fockin' starlin'!' he said, running to his van for his shotgun. The assembled multitude were then treated to McCafferty hurtling across field after field firing at any bird he saw. An innocent crow got it in the arse. 'Cam-blimey,' it croaked. At once the bookies started to call odds on his chances of success – for a while it was 7-2 on. The bangs and swearing from McCafferty continued as he gradually became a speck in the distance. Disappointed, the crowd started to drift away. Only a few aficianados remained with the odds sliding to 40 to 1. Finally he stumbled back, a 100-to-1, mud splattered, broken man.

'Here,' said Len Byrne at 5 to 1, 'let me try.' He grabbed the barrel and screaming dropped it and his odds to 20 to 1. 'Ohhhhh me hands,' he wailed, placing a burnt member under an armpit, jack-knifing up and down moaning.

'God, you'd think he'd become a Mohammdan,' said someone.

'Oh, it's bloody hot,' wailed Byrne.

The crowd, up to then bored, perked up as new betting went on to McCafferty who was going to try again. With the smell of fried eggs, he started to search every tree and bush. Blazing away, he could hear 'dat bloody starlin'' whistling in the middle of a flock of starlings which he started to chase across the country-side; firing into a bush, he peppered the legs of a pair of lovebirds. The injured lover, a six foot giant, clutched his area and chased McCafferty at 100 to 1 almost out of the county. Even there he could smell fried eggs.

(From the book *The Looney*, 1987)